PENGUIN BOOKS

Party Cakes

Party Cakes

Julie Lanham

PENGUIN BOOKS

PENGUIN BOOKS

Published by the Penguin Group
Penguin Group (Australia)
250 Camberwell Road, Camberwell, Victoria 3124, Australia
(a division of Pearson Australia Group Pty Ltd)
Penguin Group (USA) Inc.
375 Hudson Street, New York, New York 10014, USA
Penguin Group (Canada)
90 Eglinton Avenue East, Suite 700, Toronto, Canada ON M4P 2Y3
(a division of Pearson Penguin Canada Inc.)
Penguin Books Ltd
80 Strand, London WC2R 0RL England
Penguin Ireland
25 St Stephen's Green, Dublin 2, Ireland
(a division of Penguin Books Ltd)
Penguin Books India Pvt Ltd
11 Community Centre, Panchsheel Park, New Delhi – 110 017, India
Penguin Group (NZ)
67 Apollo Drive, Rosedale, North Shore 0632, New Zealand
(a division of Pearson New Zealand Ltd)
Penguin Books (South Africa) (Pty) Ltd
24 Sturdee Avenue, Rosebank, Johannesburg 2196, South Africa

Penguin Books Ltd, Registered Offices: 80 Strand, London, WC2R 0RL, England

First published by Penguin Group (Australia), 2008

10 9 8 7 6 5 4 3 2

Thanks go to Celeste and Camille Perry for their fabulous artwork.

Cover and text design by Claire Tice © Penguin Group (Australia)
Photography by Julie Renouf
Typeset in Avenir by Post Pre-press Group, Brisbane, Queensland
Colour reproduction by Splitting Image, Clayton, Victoria
Printed in China by 1010 Printing International Limited

National Library of Australia
Cataloguing-in-Publication data:

Lanham, Julie.
Party cakes.
Includes index.
ISBN 978 0 14 300814 9
1. Birthday cakes. 2. Cake decorating.
I. Title.

641.8653

penguin.com.au

Contents

Cakes

Introduction

An amazing homemade cake is a terrific way to add a sparkle to your child's birthday that will be remembered with pleasure for years to come.

Throwing a children's party can be lots of fun, and you don't need to be a whiz in the kitchen to make it a fabulous occasion. My catch cry is 'if in doubt, keep it simple'. You don't need countless dishes of food to make your party impressive – a creative, fun and delicious cake can add that extra colour to make the day a success.

Decorating a cake is such an enjoyable thing to do, so don't let the idea of it scare you – it's not as difficult as you might think, and it provides an opportunity to explore your creativity. It can be as simple or as elaborate as you like – just give it a go and enjoy yourself.

You'll have a ball deciding which cake to make, and hunting for bits and pieces to use as decorations. Rummaging through the confectionary aisle at your local supermarket, you'll rediscover all those lollies and treats you had when you were young – as well as plenty of strange and wacky new sweets to try.

Children adore birthday parties – especially when it's their own. They'll really appreciate a spectacular-looking cake that's been made especially for them. What a memory to give your child – or someone else's. And it's not only children who love fun cakes – adults are just big kids, and they'll love these birthday cakes too!

This book is full of fresh ideas, as well as new takes on some classics. It is not one of those cookbooks that's only good to look at – its aim is to inspire you to get cooking and get creative. I've included cakes of varying complexity, so there are plenty of options for both beginners and baking gurus. Children and adults alike will delight in poring over the pages, trying to decide which cake to make next.

I hope this book will continue to inspire you for years to come, and that it will help create wonderful memories for your family and friends.

Tips on cake baking

- Always read the recipe all the way through before you begin.

- Grease baking trays and tins with butter, margarine, or canola oil spray, and line the base of cake tins with non-stick baking paper.

- Pre-heat your oven to the specified temperature before baking.

- Eggs, milk and butter are best used at room temperature. The egg size used for all the recipes in this book is large (60 g). When whipping egg whites, make sure the eggs are at room temperature, and ensure the bowl you are using is scrupulously clean and dry before you begin.

- Sift dry ingredients well – this blends spices and rising agents evenly through the mixture, removes lumps, and helps incorporate air into the mixture.

- I find a hand-held electric mixer is great for making cakes – and is less cumbersome than a freestanding mixer.

- The technique to use when baking a marble cake (e.g. the Train cake on page 83) is illustrated below. Prepare the cake batter and divide into three equal portions. Colour two of the portions with cocoa or food colouring, so you have three different-coloured portions of batter (step 1). Drop spoonfuls of the batter into a prepared cake tin, alternating between the three colours (step 2). Drag a knife through the batter to create the marbled effect (step 3). Bake for the required time, or until a skewer inserted into the centre of the cake comes out clean.

Tips on cake decorating

- With any of the cake designs in this book, feel free to change the cake mixture to suit your taste. For example, if you don't like chocolate cake, use the vanilla custard cake recipe instead – just take care to match tin sizes and cooking times for different batters. I've also included a gluten-free chocolate cake recipe (page 11), which can be used for any of the birthday cakes.

- Always read decorating instructions all the way through before you begin, so you know exactly what is involved. Check the timing as well – some cakes need to be prepared a day or two in advance. (In fact, it's probably a good idea to prepare any of these cakes the day before, so you're not rushing to finish as party guests arrive.)

- Decorative cake boards are a good idea to set the cake on. They are available from party shops and cake decorating suppliers. Choose a board the same size and shape as the cake, or slightly larger, and place the cake onto it before decorating. It makes moving the cake to its final destination a lot easier.

- Before icing, you will often need to level the top of a cake. To do this, use a long bread knife to cut a thin slice from the top of the cake. Alternatively, use a long piece of dental floss – holding it taut between your hands, draw it towards you from the back of the cake to the front (you'll be amazed how well this technique works!). These techniques can also be used to cut a large cake into two layers, ready for filling.

- For best results, you need to apply a 'crumb coating' before you cover the cake with your chosen icing. This layer keeps crumbs from coming off into your topcoat of icing. The crumb coating normally consists of a thin layer of basic icing, which is left to set before the topcoat is applied.

- Keep a clean damp cloth within reach when icing cakes – use it to wipe your hands and to remove excess icing from piping tips. It's very tempting to lick your fingers, but don't give in!

- Use scissors to cut up lollies – it is much easier than using a knife. Garden secateurs are great for cutting bamboo skewers and chopsticks to length.

- Remember to use paste food colouring when colouring fondant (see also Working with fondant, pages 7–8). You can use either paste or liquid colouring to colour icings (but remember liquid colourings will thin your icing).

- If you are running short of time, you can always buy a ready-made cake to decorate. Store-bought sponges and Madeira cakes are good value.

- Toothpicks and bamboo skewers are great for holding shaped pieces of cake together and attaching decorations. But make sure you remove them before serving the cake to children!

- To make sculpting cakes easier, freeze them before shaping with a sharp knife. Freeze any cake off-cuts for later use – they're perfect for making desserts like trifle or parfait. Any extra cupcakes can be frozen, ready for lunchbox treats.

- To add sprinkles around the base of your cake, place the iced cake onto a large sheet of baking paper and pour sprinkles around the edge of the cake, then simply lift the edges of the baking paper upwards, and the sprinkles will be pressed against the base of the cake.

- Keep decorated cakes out of reach of little hands until the very last minute. The top of the fridge is a good spot.

Piping techniques

- Piping bags can be bought at supermarkets or cake-decorating shops, or you can make your own. I prefer to make my own – it's less messy and you can simply throw them away after use. It is also quick and easy to make multiple bags if you are working with more than one icing colour at a time.

- To make your own piping bags out of baking paper or cellophane, cut out a triangle measuring 30 cm across the base. Curl the paper or cellophane around to make a cone and secure with sticky tape. Fill the cone with icing, pushing it down to the point, and fold the top of the bag over several times to seal. Cut the tip off to create an opening of the size you need and use your thumb to push the icing down, while guiding the bag with your other hand.

- Alternatively, you can use a small zip-lock sandwich bag for piping. Just fill the bag with icing, then twist the top of the plastic bag to push the icing into a bottom corner. Snip a small hole in the tip and squeeze the bag to push out the icing.

- Piping tips can be used with homemade piping bags – just cut a slightly larger hole in the tip of the bag and insert the piping tip before you fill with the bag with icing.

- When working with multiple piping bags, I find the easiest way to store them when not in use is upside-down in a glass that has some damp paper towel in the bottom. This keeps mess to a minimum, and also stops the icing from drying and blocking the tip.

- In this book, I have only specified which piping tip to use when a particular type or size is required to achieve a certain look. When piping tip is not specified, just cut a hole of the necessary size in the tip of your piping bag.

TARTAN You will need two or three icing colours for this design. Attach a round tip to a piping bag and fill with the first coloured icing. Pipe vertical lines 2 cm apart; using the same colour, pipe horizontal lines 2 cm apart across the vertical lines (step 1). Attach a round tip to another piping bag and fill with the second coloured icing. Pipe vertical and horizontal lines next to the first colour (step 2). If using a third colour, attach a round tip to another piping bag and fill with that colour, then pipe vertical and horizontal lines next to the second colour (step 3). You can use different sized piping tips for each colour, if desired.

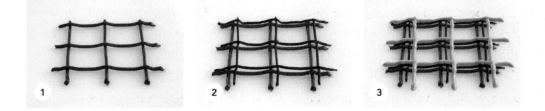

SWIRL Attach a star tip to your piping bag, then fill with icing. Hold the piping bag upright over the cake and squeeze gently. As the icing starts to appear, move the tip in a circular motion to create a swirl. Lift the tip up to break the flow of icing.

FILL-IN (TEMPLATE) METHOD Place a sheet of baking paper over the chosen template. Fill a piping bag with a small amount of royal icing (page 17) and cut a small hole in the tip. Then pipe around the outline of the template (step 1). Leave to dry before filling in. For filling in, you'll need to thin your royal icing with water to make it the consistency of runny honey. Pipe the thinned royal icing inside the outline, making sure to completely cover the design (steps 2a and 2b). Use a toothpick to move the icing into tight corners if necessary. The thinned royal icing will dry smooth. You can colour the icing before piping, or use white icing and then paint colour on once it has dried (as described on page 8). Leave decorations to dry overnight. They will dry hard but are fragile, so handle with care. Always make duplicates from your templates, in case of breakages. This technique can also be used with melted chocolate.

STAR Attach a star tip to your piping bag, then fill with icing. Hold the piping bag upright over the cake and squeeze gently. As the icing starts to appear, press down gently then lift the tip up to break the flow of icing.

CLOUDS Attach a 6-mm round tip to a piping bag and fill with icing. Hold the bag upright over the cake and squeeze gently. As the icing starts to appear, swirl the tip in a circular motion while moving the bag in a straight line (step 1). Alternate between small and large circular movements (step 2).

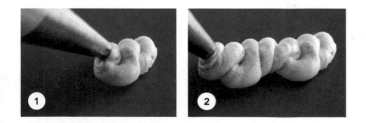

SHELL This is a great piped pattern for decorating the top and around the base of your cakes. Attach a star tip to your piping bag and fill with icing. Hold the bag on a 45-degree angle and squeeze the bag, lifting the tip as the icing begins to appear, until you have a curved mound of icing, release the pressure on the bag and drag the tip downwards to form a tapered tail. Start the next 'shell' holding the piping tip over the tapered tail of the previous one.

BASKET WEAVE Attach a basket-weave piping tip to your piping bag, then fill with icing. Pipe a horizontal line of the required length (step 1), then pipe short vertical lines across the horizontal line, leaving a gap of equal width between each (step 2). Pipe another horizontal line below the first (step 3), then pipe more short vertical lines in the spaces between the vertical lines you've already done (step 4). Repeat this pattern until the required area is filled.

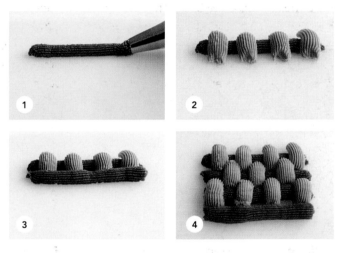

Working with fondant

- Always cover fondant with cling wrap or place it in a zip-lock bag when not in use – otherwise it will dry out.

- To make fondant workable: knead it with your hands until soft. Use immediately.

- To roll fondant: dust your work surface and rolling pin with sifted icing sugar, to stop the fondant from sticking. Knead the fondant to soften it, then flatten it slightly with your hands and roll out with the rolling pin until you reach the desired thickness.

- There are two ways to colour fondant. The first is with liquid food colouring, which softens the fondant. You can only achieve light shades using liquid colouring because you can only add small amounts or the fondant becomes too soft. The second way to colour fondant (and the way I prefer), is with paste colouring. Paste colouring doesn't soften the fondant; it allows you to create strong colours using only small amounts of colouring.

- To colour fondant: first dust your work surface with icing sugar. Then, wearing food-safe gloves to protect your hands from staining, flatten out the fondant with your hands and use a toothpick to apply the required amount of paste colouring, or add a few drops of liquid colouring. Fold each edge of the icing towards the centre, then knead and fold the fondant until you achieve an even colour. (Note that this process can be lengthy, so allow plenty of time.) If you need to colour a large amount, divide the fondant into two or three pieces and colour each separately; then knead them together before rolling out.

- To cover a cake with fondant: first apply a crumb coating of basic icing to the cake (see page 3), as this will help the fondant adhere to the cake's surface. Colour the fondant as required (step 1). Roll out the fondant to around 7 mm in thickness (or as specified), then carefully place it over the cake, gently pressing with your hands to smooth out any wrinkles (step 2). Cut off the excess and smooth the rough edges with your fingers or the back of a metal spoon.

- Add gum tragacanth powder to the fondant to make your fondant decorations dry rock hard. It can be bought from cake decorating shops.

- To paint fondant: mix paste colouring or non-toxic pastel powder with lemon essence to form a paste, and use a paintbrush to apply it to dried fondant decorations. This technique can also be used for painting royal icing decorations made using the fill-in method (page 6).

Safety tips

- Check with your doctor before consuming raw egg (as found in royal icing and mock cream). It can be unsafe for pregnant women.

- Turn pot handles in, away from the edge of stoves and bench tops, out of reach of little hands.

- Keep knives and scissors well out of reach when children are helping in the kitchen. Leave the cutting to an adult.

- Keep skewers and toothpicks out of reach of children, and make sure you remove them from cakes before serving.

- Don't use hard lollies (like gobstoppers) for cake decorations – they can be hazardous for small children, and also take a long time to eat.

ALLERGIES

- An important question to ask yourself is, 'Who is going to be eating this cake?' Allergies and food intolerances are prevalent nowadays, and it's important to accommodate everyone. Talk with the child's parent or carer and try to work out a solution; they will often have suggestions for easy ways you can adapt recipes. For example, cakes and icings that require milk can usually be made with soy milk or rice milk instead.

- When baking for children, steer well clear of any sort of nut or nut-based product. People with nut allergies can have severe reactions, which can lead to death in some cases. (Note that marzipan is made from almonds, so use buttercream icing or fondant instead).

- Opposite is a recipe for a delicious, moist gluten-free chocolate cake that can be used if you need to accommodate someone who has a gluten or wheat intolerance. (Also check that none of the decorations used for the cake contain gluten or wheat.) Alternatively, many supermarkets carry gluten-free cake mixes. The following Australian website has a variety of gluten- and wheat-free products available to purchase online: www.glutenfreeshop.com.au.

Gluten-free chocolate cake

INGREDIENTS

180 g butter

1 cup milk

1 cup rice flour

¾ cup potato flour

¾ cup arrowroot

½ cup cocoa

2 teaspoons gluten-free
   bicarbonate of soda

1½ cups white sugar

3 eggs

METHOD

Preheat oven to 180°C. Grease and line a 23-cm square cake tin.

Melt butter in a medium saucepan. Remove from heat and add milk. Sift flours, arrowroot, cocoa and bicarbonate of soda into a large bowl, then stir in sugar.

Add the milk mixture to the dry ingredients and beat until combined. Add eggs one at a time, beating well after each addition. The mixture should be light and creamy.

Pour mixture into prepared tin and bake for 40 minutes, or until a skewer inserted into the centre of the cake comes out clean.

Turn out and cool on a wire rack.

VARIATIONS

To make Texas muffins, bake for 25 minutes (makes 10).
To make cupcakes, bake for 20 minutes (makes 18).
To make mini-muffins, bake for 8 minutes (makes 48).

Shopping tips

- There are some wonderful products out there to make cake decorating easier, and most of them are really easy to get your hands on. Check out all your options in advance so you're not rushing around at the last minute.

- Department stores and the supermarket are great places to look for cake decorating inspiration. They are full of interesting lollies and other party accessories that will help make your cake and party extra special.

- Toy shops are a great source for inexpensive decorations, transfers, stickers and plastic toys. Also try your local convenience store or corner milk bar, where you can often ask for just one or two of each kind of lolly you want – just like when you were a kid!

- Two-dollar shops are also fantastic. They have heaps of ideas for themes, and plenty of cheap plastic toys, dolls, party favours and amazing lollies. Newsagents can have candles and balloons.

- Fabric and craft stores have an enormous array of inspiring products, from faux fur to biscuit cutters.

- For more specialised cake decorating tools and ingredients, try a cake decorating shop. They stock a range of extras like pre-made icing flowers, cute candles and cake boards. Also have a look at homewares shops for baking tins, utensils and cake stands.

- And remember to check out party supplies shops. They often have a great range of lollies, balloons, cake boards, cake decorations and candles.

- There's a list of cake decorating suppliers on page 235, but it's also a good idea to have a look in your local phone book. You never know, there may be a cake decorating shop just around the corner!

Icing recipes

Buttercream icing

Buttercream is such a versatile icing. It can be easily coloured, makes a great cake filling, and will hold its shape when piped (prepare to a thick consistency when using for piping). Make sure you use unsalted butter as it gives a much better flavour.

INGREDIENTS

250 g softened unsalted butter

1 x 500-g packet pure icing sugar

3 tablespoons milk

food colouring (optional)

METHOD

Cream butter until light and fluffy. Continue beating while gradually adding sifted icing sugar.

Add milk a little at a time, beating until smooth. (Add a little more or a little less milk, to achieve the desired consistency.)

Add food colouring a little at a time (if using), mixing until you have an even colour.

NOTE This icing needs to be refrigerated, and any cake that has been iced with buttercream should also be refrigerated. Remove the cake from the fridge 30 minutes before serving, to bring it to room temperature.

Chocolate buttercream icing

Sometimes it just has to be chocolate, and this is a great basic chocolate icing recipe for icing and decorating cakes.

INGREDIENTS

1 x 500-g packet pure icing sugar

¼ cup cocoa

250 g softened unsalted butter

3 tablespoons milk

METHOD

Sift together icing sugar and cocoa.

In a separate bowl, cream butter until light and fluffy. Continue beating while gradually adding icing sugar mixture.

Add milk a little at a time, beating until smooth. (Add a little more or a little less milk, to achieve the desired consistency.)

NOTE This icing needs to be refrigerated, and any cake that has been iced with chocolate buttercream should also be refrigerated. Remove the cake from the fridge 30 minutes before serving, to bring it to room temperature.

Basic icing

This icing is primarily used for crumb coating, as well as for securing decorations and fondant onto cakes. It can also be coloured and used for icing cakes. To use for piping, prepare to a thick consistency.

INGREDIENTS

1 x 500-g packet pure icing sugar

2 teaspoons unsalted butter, melted

2 tablespoons hot water

food colouring (optional)

METHOD

Sift icing sugar into a bowl. Add butter and beat while gradually adding hot water. (Add a little more or a little less water, to achieve the desired consistency.)

Add food colouring a little at a time (if using), mixing until you have an even colour.

Mock cream

This is a very rich buttercream. It can be used to achieve a smooth finish when icing cakes and is also good for piping decorations. It can be a little tricky to make, so some patience is required to get good results – but it is well worth the effort!

INGREDIENTS

250 g white sugar

½ cup water

6 egg whites

320 g unsalted butter, diced

1 teaspoon vanilla extract

food colouring (optional)

METHOD

Heat sugar and water in a heavy-based saucepan and bring to the boil. Continue boiling and use a pastry brush dipped in cold water to occasionally brush sugar crystals off the sides of the pan. Boil for about 7 minutes, until the syrup reaches 'soft ball' stage (when a small amount of the sugar syrup dropped into chilled water forms a soft and flexible ball, or when a candy thermometer reads 118–120°C).

Whip the egg whites until stiff peaks form.

Slowly add the sugar syrup to the egg whites in a thin stream while beating continuously. Beat until the outside of the bowl feels cool (about 10 minutes).

Continue to beat while gradually adding the butter. Reduce speed and add vanilla and food colouring (if using). (Don't worry if it looks curdled, just keep beating until it becomes creamy.)

Royal icing

Royal icing is terrific for piping, and is perfect for fill-in (template) work as it dries very hard. It can be coloured during preparation, or left white and then painted with food colouring once set.

INGREDIENTS

2 egg whites

2 teaspoons fresh lemon juice

1 x 500-g packet pure icing sugar

food colouring (optional)

METHOD

Combine egg whites and lemon juice in a large bowl. Sift in icing sugar. Add food colouring (if using).

Beat on low speed for about 5 minutes, until mixture is thick and stiff.

This icing will keep for up to 1 week in the fridge. To store: transfer to a plastic container, drape a damp cloth over the top, then seal with the lid.

NOTE To use royal icing for fill-in work: dilute the icing with a small amount of water until it is the consistency of runny honey. To paint colour onto white royal icing: wait until it has set, then mix your chosen paste colouring or non-toxic pastel powder with a little lemon essence and paint on with a fine paintbrush.

Big bikkie

CHOC-CHIP BISCUIT

125 g softened butter

1 cup soft brown sugar

1 egg

1 teaspoon vanilla extract

2½ cups self-raising flour

1 cup large dark chocolate chips, plus extra for decorating

5-cm round biscuit cutter

METHOD

Preheat oven to 180°C. Place a 20-cm round cake tin onto a sheet of baking paper and trace around the tin with a pencil. Place the baking paper upside-down on a baking tray. Repeat with a second sheet of baking paper.

Cream butter and sugar until light and fluffy. Add egg and vanilla extract and beat well. Add sifted flour and beat to combine. Fold in choc chips.

Spoon mixture into the two circles on the prepared trays and spread out, leaving a 2-cm border between outline and dough to allow for spreading.

Place some extra chocolate chips onto the top of each biscuit. Bake for about 20 minutes, or until golden.

Remove biscuits from the oven. Leave on the baking trays and while still hot use the round biscuit cutter to cut three bite marks out of one edge of each biscuit. Leave on the baking trays to cool.

NOTE These biscuits break easily, which is why it's best to bake two, even though only one is needed for the cake.

continued

VANILLA CUSTARD CAKE

250 g softened butter

1½ cups white sugar

3 eggs

¾ cup custard powder

2 cups self-raising flour

½ cup milk

2 teaspoons vanilla extract

DECORATION

1 round vanilla custard cake (above)

1 choc-chip biscuit (page 19)

1 quantity chocolate buttercream icing (page 14)

large white chocolate chips

METHOD

Preheat oven to 180°C. Grease and line a 20-cm round cake tin.

Cream butter and sugar until light and fluffy. Add eggs one at a time, beating well after each addition.

Gradually add sifted custard powder and flour and beat well. Beat in milk and vanilla extract until combined.

Pour batter into prepared tin and bake for 45 minutes, or until a skewer inserted into the centre of the cake comes out clean.

Turn out and cool on a wire rack.

ASSEMBLY

Level the top of the vanilla custard cake and carefully slide the cooled biscuit on top. Use a sharp knife to cut three bite shapes out of the cake, to match those in the biscuit. Carefully slide the biscuit off the cake.

Place the cake onto a cake board and ice all over with chocolate icing. Carefully place the biscuit back on top of the cake, positioning the bites so they line up.

Decorate the sides of the cake with the large white chocolate chips.

Boat

CHOCOLATE CAKES

220 g butter

2 cups milk

3 cups self-raising flour

1 cup cocoa

2 cups white sugar

3 eggs

1 teaspoon vanilla extract

METHOD

Preheat oven to 180°C. Lightly grease and line two 23-cm square cake tins.

Gently heat butter and milk in a saucepan until butter is melted. Set aside.

Sift flour and cocoa into a large bowl. Add sugar, eggs and vanilla extract and beat until well combined. Gradually add milk mixture, beating until thick and smooth.

Pour batter into prepared tins. Bake for 45 minutes, or until a skewer inserted into the centre comes out clean.

Turn out and cool on wire racks.

continued

DECORATION

2 square chocolate cakes
(page 21)

templates (pages 200–1)

1 quantity basic icing (page 15)

lollies: cola sour straps

1 quantity buttercream icing
(page 13)

food colouring: black, red,
blue, green

ready-made icing letters
(e.g. Cake Mate alphabet)

ASSEMBLY

Level the tops of the two chocolate cakes, then use the templates provided to cut the required shapes from the cake. Crumb coat each shape with basic icing and leave to set.

Use scissors to cut out eight 2-cm rounds from the cola sour straps, for the portholes.

Divide buttercream into four medium bowls and one small bowl. Colour the small portion black and place into a piping bag. Set aside. Leave one of the larger portions plain, and colour each of the remaining three a different colour – red, blue and green.

Ice a cake board with the blue buttercream, to represent the water. Ice the hull (bottom) boat cake piece with red buttercream, then carefully position it onto the cake board.

Ice the deck (middle) boat cake piece with green buttercream. Carefully place on top of the red piece. Pipe a thin outline of black buttercream around the top edge of the green piece. Using icing letters, stick the child's name and age onto the side of the green cake, near the front (as shown in the photograph).

Ice the cabin (top) cake piece with plain buttercream, then place on top of the green piece. Pipe an outline of black buttercream around the top edge of the cabin and stick four cola sour portholes along each side.

Ice the two smokestacks with red buttercream, then pipe a black stripe around each (as shown). Carefully place the smokestacks on top of the white cabin.

Up the garden path

One day before: make royal icing and fondant decorations
On the day: bake cake and assemble

VANILLA CUSTARD CAKE

250 g softened butter

1½ cups white sugar

3 eggs

¾ cup custard powder

2 cups self-raising flour

½ cup milk

2 teaspoons vanilla extract

METHOD

Preheat oven to 180°C. Grease and line a 23-cm square cake tin.

Cream butter and sugar until light and fluffy. Add eggs one at a time, beating well after each addition.

Gradually add sifted custard powder and flour and beat well. Beat in milk and vanilla extract until combined.

Pour batter into prepared tin and bake for 40 minutes, or until a skewer inserted into the centre of the cake comes out clean.

Turn out and cool on a wire rack.

continued

DECORATION

1 quantity royal icing (page 17)

food colouring: orange, green, blue, lime-green, pink, purple, brown, black

templates (page 202)

2 × 500-g packets white fondant

1 × 500-g packet chocolate fondant

floristry wire

1 square vanilla custard cake (page 25)

1 quantity basic icing (page 15)

ASSEMBLY

Divide the royal icing into eight small bowls and colour each portion a different colour – orange, green, blue, lime-green, pink, purple, brown and black. Place each colour into a separate piping bag.

Place a sheet of baking paper over the templates provided and use the royal icing to make flowers, grass, butterflies, bees and ants (see fill-in technique on page 6). Make three or four of each. Store all leftover royal icing in the fridge for later use.

Roll out one packet of white fondant to 6 mm in thickness. Cut out the fence using a pizza cutter or sharp knife, as follows. For the horizontal beams, cut out strips 15 mm wide and the same length as the sides of the cake – cut out two beams for each side. Then cut out 36 pickets using the template provided. Colour the leftover fondant brown and roll it into four balls of varying sizes. Shape these into flower pots (as shown in the photograph opposite).

Take a walnut-sized piece of white fondant from the second packet and roughly knead it into the chocolate fondant. Make around 20 small balls from this fondant, reducing the size of the balls as you go. Flatten each ball with your hands, to make stones for the garden path. Make four more flat rounds to fit into the top of each flower pot as dirt. Leave royal icing and fondant decorations to dry overnight.

Cut about 12 lengths of floristry wire and use royal icing to stick a piece onto the back of some of the flowers, bees and butterflies. Leave to set.

Level the top of the vanilla custard cake and crumb coat with basic icing. Colour remaining white fondant green, roll out to 7 mm in thickness and use to cover the cake.

Arrange royal icing and fondant decorations on top of the cake, using the picture as a guide. Lastly, use royal icing to stick the fence onto the front of the cake and the grass and some of the flowers and ants onto the fence. If desired, use any leftover green royal icing to pipe some more grass onto the fence.

Strawberry-ripple heart

CHOCOLATE HEART CAKE

110 g butter

1 cup milk

1½ cups self-raising flour

½ cup cocoa

1 cup white sugar

2 eggs

½ teaspoon vanilla extract

METHOD

Preheat oven to 180°C. Grease and line a deep 23-cm heart cake tin.

Gently heat butter and milk in a saucepan until butter is melted. Set aside.

Sift flour and cocoa into a large bowl. Add sugar, eggs and vanilla extract and beat until well combined. Gradually add milk mixture, beating until thick and smooth.

Pour batter into prepared tin and bake for 45 minutes, or until a skewer inserted into the centre of the cake comes out clean.

Turn out and cool on a wire rack.

continued

DECORATION

1 chocolate heart cake (page 29)

500 g white cooking chocolate, chopped

oil-based powder colouring: pink, red

pink lustre dust

2 litres vanilla ice-cream

deep 23-cm heart cake tin

1 × 450-g jar strawberry jam

300 ml thickened cream

pink sprinkles

ASSEMBLY

Cut the chocolate heart cake in half horizontally, to make two layers.

Place 200 grams of the white chocolate in a microwave-safe bowl and heat on MEDIUM for 20 seconds at a time, stirring between bursts, until melted and smooth. Once melted, add pink chocolate colouring and stir until an even colour. Place into a piping bag (reserving a few spoonfuls for later use). Pipe about 200 1-cm dots onto a sheet of baking paper. Leave to set. Once set, brush each chocolate dot with pink lustre dust.

Remove ice-cream from freezer and set aside to soften for 10 minutes. (Remember that when using ice-cream, it's important to work quickly and refreeze the ice-cream as soon as possible. If the ice-cream starts to melt, return to the freezer for a few minutes.)

Line the heart tin with cling wrap, leaving plenty of excess overhanging. Place one of the cake layers into the bottom of the tin. Cover the cake with a 2-cm layer of ice-cream, using the back of a spoon to level the surface. Dollop spoonfuls of strawberry jam over the ice-cream layer. Cover with another layer of ice-cream and jam. Repeat this process until the ice-cream is 3 cm from the top of the tin. Smooth the final layer of ice-cream with the back of a metal spoon.

Place remaining cake layer cut-side down on top of the ice-cream layer. Press down gently, making sure the top of the cake is flat. Completely cover the top of the cake with the overhanging cling wrap. Refreeze for at least 2 hours.

To make red ganache, bring the thickened cream to the boil over low heat. Remove from the heat and add the reserved 300 grams of chocolate, stirring until the chocolate has melted. Add red chocolate colouring and stir until evenly blended. Set aside to cool until the chocolate mixture is beginning to harden but is still creamy in texture.

Remove the cake from the freezer and carefully turn out onto a cake board. Remove cling wrap. Working quickly and carefully, coat the cake with the red ganache. Make sure the ganache is smooth and that all of the cake and ice-cream is covered. While ganache is still wet, cover the sides of the cake with pink sprinkles. Return cake to the freezer for 1 hour.

Re-melt the reserved pink chocolate in the microwave and use it to adhere the pink chocolate dots to the top of the cake. Return cake to the freezer until ready to serve.

Caterpillar

VANILLA CUSTARD CUPCAKES

250 g softened butter

1½ cups white sugar

3 eggs

¾ cup custard powder

2 cups self-raising flour

½ cup milk

2 teaspoons vanilla extract

METHOD

Preheat oven to 180°C. Line two regular muffin pans with 18 cupcake papers.

Cream butter and sugar until light and fluffy. Add eggs one at a time, beating well after each addition.

Gradually add sifted custard powder and flour and beat well. Beat in milk and vanilla extract until combined.

Divide batter into cupcake papers and bake for about 20 minutes, or until a skewer inserted into the centre of a cupcake comes out clean. Turn cupcakes out onto a wire rack to cool.

NOTE You will only need ten cupcakes for the caterpillar cake, so freeze the rest for later use.

continued

DECORATION

1 quantity buttercream icing
(page 13)

food colouring: red, blue,
green

10 vanilla custard cupcakes
(page 33)

1 quantity basic icing (page 15)

lollies: 1 white marshmallow,
1 orange sour strap,
1 liquorice stick, cola sour
straps, green apple sour tubes

silver cachous

orange sprinkles

ASSEMBLY

Divide the buttercream icing into two small bowls and
one large bowl. Colour one of the small portions red
and the other blue. Colour the large portion light-green.

Use 1 cup of the light-green icing to cover a cake board.

Remove the cupcake papers from all the cooled
cupcakes. Cut the tops off seven of the cupcakes (steps
1a and 1b), then slice about 1 cm off one side of each of
them (step 2). Place cut-side down (step 3). Crumb coat
each of these cupcakes with basic icing and leave to set.
These will make the body of the caterpillar.

Cut another cupcake in half vertically. Place one half cut-side down in the centre of the cake board; discard the other half. Take another cupcake and trim 15 mm off the edges on two opposite sides; discard the centre piece. Place these pieces on either side of the larger piece (step 1). Cover all three pieces with light-green buttercream. This is the mound the caterpillar is crawling over.

Colour the remaining green buttercream a darker shade of green and use it to ice each body piece. Arrange the seven body pieces on the cake board, with cut-sides facing down and flat sides touching: place one piece on each side of the mound, and three on top of the mound (step 2). Place the last two on the right-hand side (step 3). Secure with toothpicks if necessary.

Ice the remaining whole cupcake with red buttercream for the head. Position at the left-hand end of the body with the muffin top facing forwards (as shown in the main photograph).

To make the eyes, cut a white marshmallow in half horizontally. Then use scissors to cut two rounds out of the orange sour straps, slightly smaller in diameter than the marshmallow slices. Cut two thin slices from the liquorice stick. Use a little icing to stick each liquorice round onto an orange sour strap round, then stick each orange round onto a white marshmallow round. Stick the eyes onto the head of the caterpillar. Cut a small triangle from the remaining liquorice for the nose and stick it on.

Use the remaining red buttercream to ice a red spot on top of each of the caterpillar's 'humps'. Place the blue buttercream into a piping bag, pipe a blue spiral of icing onto each red spot and some small blue dots of icing onto the side of the caterpillar, then stick a silver cachou onto each of these dots. Use the blue icing to pipe the mouth of the caterpillar (as shown in the photograph on page 36).

continued

Sprinkle some orange sprinkles onto each of the caterpillar's humps. Cut the apple sour tubes into strips for the grass and place them around the sides of the caterpillar.

Cut the cola sour straps into about 20 triangles for the legs and stick them onto the sides of the caterpillar. Also cut out antennae from the cola sour straps and stick them onto the head (as shown below).

Puppy

One day before: bake cakes and assemble (this cake is time-consuming to make)

CHOCOLATE CAKES

220 g butter

2 cups milk

3 cups self-raising flour

1 cup cocoa

2 cups white sugar

3 eggs

1 teaspoon vanilla extract

METHOD

Preheat oven to 180°C. Grease one cup of a Texas muffin pan, four cups of a mini muffin pan, then grease and line a 25-cm × 11.5-cm loaf tin.

Gently heat butter and milk in a saucepan until butter is melted. Set aside.

Sift flour and cocoa into a large bowl. Add sugar, eggs and vanilla extract and beat until well combined. Gradually add milk mixture, beating until thick and smooth.

Divide batter into one Texas muffin cup, four mini muffin cups, and the loaf tin. Bake the mini muffins for 8 minutes, the Texas muffin for 25 minutes, and the loaf cake for 45 minutes, or until a skewer inserted into the centre comes out clean.

Turn out and cool on wire racks.

continued

DECORATION

1 chocolate loaf cake (page 37)

1 chocolate Texas muffin
(page 37)

4 mini chocolate muffins
(page 37)

½ quantity basic icing (page 15)

2 × 500-g packets white
fondant

2-cm round biscuit cutter

food colouring: pink, black

1 × 500-g packet chocolate
fondant

template (page 203)

2 bamboo skewers

toothpicks

½ quantity royal icing (page 17)

ASSEMBLY

Cut a quarter off the end of the loaf cake and discard.
Round the edges of the remaining piece with a sharp
knife, this will be the body. Round the edges of the
Texas muffin, for the head. The mini muffins will be
the legs. Crumb coat each piece with basic icing.

Roll out the white fondant to 5 mm in thickness and use
it to cover the body, head and each mini muffin, securing
with a little basic icing. Using the biscuit cutter, cut out
two rounds for the eyes. Roll a ball of white fondant that
is 5 cm in diameter for the snout, and cut a slice into it
for the mouth. Set aside to dry.

Colour a small amount of the white fondant pink for the
tongue; roll out and cut a tongue-shape that is about
15 mm wide and 3 cm long. Colour a small amount of
white fondant black for the nose; roll into a ball about
15 mm in diameter.

Roll out the chocolate fondant to 5 mm in thickness.
Cut out two rounds 15 cm in diameter, and one round
6 cm in diameter. Use basic icing to stick the two larger
spots onto the dog's body, and the smaller spot onto the
head (as shown in the photograph). Using the template
provided, cut out two ears from the chocolate fondant,
and stick onto the head with basic icing.

For the tail, roll a snake 2 cm wide and 12 cm long from
the chocolate fondant. Taper the tail at one end, and
push a bamboo skewer into the other end, until it
reaches about halfway up the tail. Set aside to dry.

continued

Place the four mini muffins onto a cake board, for the legs. Dab a little basic icing onto the top of each leg and stick a toothpick into each top, leaving half of each toothpick sticking out. Position the body onto the mini muffins (as shown in the photograph) and press down gently.

Cut a skewer in half. Push one of the pieces into the base of the head, leaving half sticking out. Gently push the head into position on the dog. Push the tail into the body.

Coat the back of the snout with a little basic icing, press a toothpick into it and then press the snout into the head. Use basic icing to stick the eyes and tongue onto the face. Place a little basic icing on the back of the nose, press a toothpick into it and gently press the nose into the snout.

Colour the royal icing black and place into a piping bag. Pipe the detail onto each eye and onto the snout (as shown in the photograph).

Leave cake to dry overnight.

Pirate ship

 One day before: make the ship's masts and sails
On the day: bake cake and assemble

CHOCOLATE CAKE

110 g butter

1 cup milk

1½ cups self-raising flour

½ cup cocoa

1 cup white sugar

2 eggs

½ teaspoon vanilla extract

METHOD

Preheat oven to 180°C. Grease and line a 23-cm square cake tin.

Gently heat butter and milk in a saucepan until butter is melted. Set aside.

Sift flour and cocoa into a large bowl. Add sugar, eggs and vanilla extract and beat until well combined. Gradually add milk mixture, beating until thick and smooth.

Pour batter into prepared tin and bake for 45 minutes, or until a skewer inserted into the centre of the cake comes out clean.

Turn out and cool on a wire rack.

continued

ASSEMBLY

Using the brown marker pen, colour the chopsticks all over. To make the tall mast, use secateurs to cut one chopstick in half, then glue one half to the tapered end of another chopstick.

Fold the calico in half to make a rectangle measuring 20 cm × 60 cm. Iron it flat to make a crease down the centre, then open the fabric out. Place the Visofix paper-side up onto the fabric, positioning it to line up with the crease and cover half the fabric. Iron over the paper, then peel it off once the interfacing has stuck to the calico. Carefully fold the calico in half at the crease, covering the Visofix, then iron until it adheres to the bottom piece of calico.

Use the templates provided to cut out the three sails from the calico. Stick pieces of double-sided sticky tape down the centre of each sail, then attach the largest and smallest sail to the long chopstick, and the medium sail to the shorter chopstick. Set aside.

Place about 2 tablespoons of the white buttercream into a piping bag. To the remaining white buttercream add 2 tablespoons of sifted cocoa and mix in.

Level the top of the chocolate cake, then use the template provided to cut out the required ship shapes from the cake.

continued

From the cake off-cuts: cut out four pieces measuring 2 cm high × 2 cm wide × 4 cm long, for the sides of the deck; then cut out a piece 2 cm high × 2 cm wide × 6 cm long, to fit across the back of the ship, on top of the stern piece you've already cut. Arrange cake pieces on the cake board, starting with the hull (bottom level), then place bow and stern pieces on top. Finally, position the side pieces and extra back piece. Secure together with bamboo skewers. Crumb coat the entire cake with basic icing and set aside to dry.

Once crumb coat has set, ice the whole cake with the chocolate buttercream. Use the white buttercream to pipe an outline around the top of the cake (as shown in the photograph).

Cut the liquorice straps into various lengths to make planks and arrange along the sides of the ship. Use scissors to cut 2-cm squares from the cola sour straps to make windows and gun turrets, and stick onto the ship. Use slices of liquorice stick for the canons.

Gently push the masts into the cake.

Crown

One day before: make fondant parts of crown and fondant tassels
On the day: bake cake, sew fabric parts of crown, and assemble

VANILLA CUSTARD CAKE

250 g softened butter

1½ cups white sugar

3 eggs

¾ cup custard powder

2 cups self-raising flour

½ cup milk

2 teaspoons vanilla extract

METHOD

Preheat oven to 180°C. Grease and line a 23-cm square cake tin.

Cream butter and sugar until light and fluffy. Add eggs one at a time, beating well after each addition.

Gradually add sifted custard powder and flour and beat well. Beat in milk and vanilla extract until combined.

Pour batter into prepared tin and bake for 40 minutes, or until a skewer inserted into the centre of the cake comes out clean.

Turn out and cool on a wire rack.

continued

ASSEMBLY

Roll out one packet of white fondant to 5 mm in thickness. Cut a long 2-cm wide strip. Cut the bottom off the lemonade bottle, set it cut-side down on your work surface and wrap the fondant strip around it, trimming to fit and securing the join with a little royal icing.

Using the cutters, cut out ten 2-cm flowers, ten 3-cm flowers, and 20 leaves from the rolled fondant.

To assemble the crown: stick the fondant flowers and leaves onto the band of fondant that is wrapped around the bottle, as follows. First, secure the large flowers to the front of the crown with a little royal icing, the petals of each flower just touching. Then stick the leaves and small flowers around the top of the crown, alternating between the two. Leave fondant crown to dry overnight. (Store leftover royal icing in the fridge for later use.)

To make the tassels using the second packet of white fondant, roll 60 strands measuring 5 cm long and 2 mm thick. Gather 15 of these strands together in a bunch and press together at one end. Repeat for remaining strands. Roll out remaining fondant from this packet to 3 mm in thickness and cut out four 1-cm wide strips. Wrap one strip around the end of each bunch of strands, trim any excess and use a little water to stick on. Roll four 1-cm balls from fondant, brush with a little water and stick one on the end of each bunch of strands. Use a paintbrush to dust each tassel with silver lustre dust. Leave to dry overnight.

Round the edges of the vanilla custard cake and cut out a small indent in the centre. Then create two long indents, 1 cm deep, running diagonally across the cake from corner to corner, to form a cross. Crumb coat the cake with basic icing.

To make the cushion: colour the third packet of fondant green, roll out to 7 mm in thickness and cover the cake, securing with some royal icing. Make sure to push the fondant down into the indentations to form creases.

Scrape some powder from the green pastel into a dish and add a little lemon essence. Mix to a paste, and use this to paint the creases. Leave to dry. Then use a paintbrush to apply green pearl dust over the cushion. Use a paintbrush to apply silver lustre dust to the creases and edges of the cushion. Place the cushion onto a cake board.

Carefully lift the bottle up out of the fondant crown. Paint the crown with silver lustre dust.

Put remaining royal icing into a piping bag and pipe small dots all around the edge of the cake (as shown in the photograph). Stick a silver cachou onto each dot. Use royal icing to stick a tassel onto each corner of the cushion.

Cut a 20-cm circle out of the square of pink velvet. Using a gathering stitch on your sewing machine, sew around the edge of the circle. Gently pull the threads until the edges pull in. Put a little scrunched tissue paper inside to fill out the velvet.

Measure around the outside of the fondant crown and cut the faux fur to measure the same width.

continued

Roll fur into a long sausage, with furry side on the outside. Use a running stitch on your machine to sew the join together, then sew the ends together.

Attach the velvet to the ring of fur by tacking in a few places. Position in the centre of the cushion and carefully place the crown on top of the fur, using a skewer to manoeuvre the velvet into place (as shown in the photograph).

Marmalade cat

🕐 **One day before:** bake cakes and assemble (this cake is time-consuming to make)

CHOCOLATE CAKES

220 g butter

2 cups milk

3 cups self-raising flour

1 cup cocoa

2 cups white sugar

3 eggs

1 teaspoon vanilla extract

METHOD

Preheat oven to 180°C. Grease one cup of a regular muffin pan, one cup of a Texas muffin pan, two cups of a mini muffin pan, then grease and line a 25-cm × 11.5-cm loaf tin.

Gently heat butter and milk in a saucepan until butter is melted. Set aside.

Sift flour and cocoa into a large bowl. Add sugar, eggs and vanilla extract and beat until well combined. Gradually add milk mixture, beating until thick and smooth.

Divide batter into one regular muffin cup, one Texas muffin cup, two mini-muffin cups and the loaf tin. Bake the mini muffins for 8 minutes, the Texas muffin for 25 minutes, and the loaf cake for 45 minutes, or until a skewer inserted into the centre comes out clean.

Turn out and cool on wire racks.

continued

1 chocolate loaf cake (page 51)

1 chocolate Texas muffin
 (page 51)

1 regular chocolate muffin
 (page 51)

2 mini chocolate muffins
 (page 51)

1 quantity basic icing (page 15)

2 × 500-g packets white
 fondant

food colouring: red, blue, pink,
 yellow, brown, black

2-cm round biscuit cutter

1-cm round piping tip

templates (page 205)

bamboo skewers

¼ quantity royal icing (page 17)

toothpicks

1 × packet sour strawberry
 spaghetti

ASSEMBLY

Cut a quarter off the end of the loaf cake and discard. Round the edges of the remaining piece; this will be the body. Round the edges of the Texas muffin for the head. Round the edges of the regular muffin for the ball of wool. The mini muffins will be for the legs. Crumb coat each piece with basic icing.

Take an egg-sized piece from the first packet of white fondant and colour it red. Use this to make a 2-cm ball for the nose, then roll out the remainder to 5 mm in thickness and use to cover the regular muffin. Set aside to dry.

Roll out remainder of the first packet of fondant, cut out two rounds with the biscuit cutter for the whites of the eyes. Colour a pea-sized piece of fondant light-blue; roll out to 5 mm in thickness and use the piping tip to cut out two 1-cm rounds for the pupils.

Colour a marble-sized piece of fondant pink and roll it out to 5 mm in thickness. Use the template provided to cut out the shape for the insides of the ears.

Combine remaining white fondant from the first packet with the second packet of fondant, then divide into two even pieces. Colour one portion yellow and the other portion brown. Roughly combine the two portions, then roll out to 7 mm in thickness.

Use the marbled fondant to cover the body, head and legs, securing with basic icing. From the same fondant, roll a snake 2 cm wide and 15 cm long to make the tail. Taper at one end, push a bamboo skewer into the other end until it reaches about halfway up the tail. Based on the template provided, cut two ears out of this fondant. Use royal icing to stick the insides of the ears onto the ears.

Position the body on the cake board. Cut a bamboo skewer in half. Push one of the pieces into the base of the head, leaving half sticking out. Gently push the head into position on the cat. Push the tail into the body.

Place a little royal icing on the back of the nose, press a toothpick into it and then gently press the nose into the head. Use royal icing to stick on the eyes and ears.

Colour one spoonful of royal icing red and another spoonful black. Place into separate piping bags and pipe on the whiskers and the mouth (as shown in the photograph).

Cover the red ball with the strawberry spaghetti. Position this ball of wool in front of the cat and drape a piece of strawberry spaghetti over the cat's back. Dab a little royal icing onto each leg, then stick a toothpick into each leg, leaving half sticking out. Position the legs as shown in the photograph, gently pushing them into the body.

Leave cake to dry overnight.

Princess

VANILLA CUSTARD LOAF CAKE

- 250 g softened butter
- 1½ cups white sugar
- 3 eggs
- ¾ cup custard powder
- 2 cups self-raising flour
- ½ cup milk
- 2 teaspoons vanilla extract

METHOD

Preheat oven to 180°C. Lightly grease and line a 25-cm × 11.5-cm loaf tin.

Cream butter and sugar until light and fluffy. Add eggs one at a time, beating well after each addition.

Gradually add sifted custard powder and flour and beat well. Beat in milk and vanilla extract until combined.

Pour batter into prepared loaf tin and bake for 45 minutes, or until a skewer inserted into the centre of the cake comes out clean.

Turn out and cool on a wire rack.

continued

DECORATION

1 vanilla custard loaf cake
(page 55)

templates (page 206)

½ quantity basic icing (page 15)

1 × 500-g packet white fondant

food colouring: cream, pink

20-cm length of 1-cm wide pink
satin ribbon

15-cm length white tulle
(off the roll)

toothpicks

double-sided sticky tape

40-cm length of 1-cm wide
pink grosgrain ribbon

small glass pedestal cake stand

½ quantity royal icing (page 17)

silver cachous

mini plastic crown

ASSEMBLY

Trim one end of the vanilla custard loaf cake to level it; this end will be the base. Then use the template provided to cut the torso shape from the cake. Crumb coat with basic icing and set aside to dry.

Colour one third of the fondant with cream food colouring and roll out to 7 mm in thickness. Cover the top third of the cake with the fondant, securing it with basic icing and smoothing out any wrinkles.

Cut the 20-cm length of 1-cm wide pink satin ribbon in half and drape a piece over each 'shoulder' of the cake. Secure with basic icing.

Colour the remaining fondant pink and roll out to 7 mm in thickness. Using the template provided, cut out the bodice shape from the fondant and carefully secure onto the cake with basic icing (as shown in the photograph). Smooth out any wrinkles as you go and trim any excess around the base. Carefully cut off any excess fondant at the back of the cake and join the two edges together.

Sew the piece of tulle across its width using a gathering stitch on your sewing machine. Pull the threads to gather up the tulle – gather enough so that the tulle measures the same as the 'waist' of the cake. Carefully place the tutu around the base of the cake and secure at the back with toothpicks.

Stick a piece of double-sided tape around the waist, covering the top of the tutu and attach the grosgrain ribbon to this. Tie a big bow at the back. Place the cake onto the cake stand.

Put the royal icing into a piping bag and pipe small dots around the top of the bodice (as shown). Stick a silver cachou onto each dot. Finally, place the mini plastic crown over one shoulder.

Basketball

VANILLA CUSTARD PUDDING CAKES

250 g softened butter

1½ cups white sugar

3 eggs

¾ cup custard powder

2 cups self-raising flour

½ cup milk

2 teaspoons vanilla extract

METHOD

Preheat oven to 180°C. Grease two 15-cm pudding tins.

Cream butter and sugar until light and fluffy. Add eggs one at a time, beating well after each addition.

Gradually add sifted custard powder and flour and beat well. Beat in milk and vanilla extract until combined.

Pour batter into prepared tins and bake for 40 minutes, or until a skewer inserted into the centre comes out clean.

Turn out and cool on wire racks.

continued

**2 vanilla custard pudding cakes
(page 59)**

**1 quantity buttercream icing
(page 13)**

1 × 500-g packet white fondant

food colouring: orange

2-mm round piping tip

lollies: liquorice straps

ASSEMBLY

Join the two pudding cakes together with buttercream icing, to form a ball. Trim the edges of the cake with a sharp knife to make a perfectly round shape. Crumb coat with buttercream icing.

Colour the packet of white fondant orange. Roll out to 5 mm in thickness and use to cover the ball, securing with extra buttercream if needed. Use the piping tip to stipple indentations all over the basketball, mimicking the texture of a real basketball. Place cake onto a cake board.

Cut four long thin strips from the liquorice straps. Position the liquorice strips over the ball (as shown in the photograph), securing with a little buttercream.

Bee cupcakes

CHOCOLATE CUPCAKES

220 g butter

2 cups milk

3 cups self-raising flour

1 cup cocoa

2 cups white sugar

3 eggs

1 teaspoon vanilla extract

METHOD

Preheat oven to 180°C. Line three regular muffin pans with 30 brown cupcake papers.

Gently heat butter and milk in a saucepan until butter is melted. Set aside.

Sift flour and cocoa into a large bowl. Add sugar, eggs and vanilla extract and beat until well combined. Gradually add milk mixture, beating until thick and smooth.

Divide batter into cupcake papers and bake for 20 minutes, or until a skewer inserted into the centre of a cupcake comes out clean.

Turn out and cool on wire racks.

continued

ASSEMBLY

Place a sheet of baking paper over the wings template provided. Put eight white chocolate buttons in a small microwave-safe bowl and heat on MEDIUM for 10 seconds at a time, stirring between bursts, until melted and smooth. Colour the melted chocolate yellow, place into a piping bag and, working quickly, pipe outlines of wings onto the baking paper (see fill-in method on page 6). Melt and colour more batches of white chocolate if necessary. Continue until you have about 20 pairs of wings (to allow for some breakages).

Melt another batch of eight chocolate buttons and put into a clean piping bag. Fill in the wing outlines with white chocolate. Melt more chocolate if necessary.

Place a sheet of baking paper over the flower template provided. Melt another batch of chocolate and colour it pink. Place into a piping bag and outline the flowers. When dry, fill in with more pink chocolate. Continue until you have ten pink flowers. Repeat this process to make ten blue flowers. Melt another batch of chocolate and colour it yellow. Pipe a blob into the centre of each flower.

For this cake, half the chocolate Royals will be decorated as bees, and the other half with flowers. For the 15 bees, melt another batch of chocolate and colour it yellow. Put into a piping bag and pipe four or five stripes across each chocolate biscuit (as shown in the photograph).

continued

For the eyes, pipe two small dots onto the front of each biscuit and stick a gold cachou onto each dot. Carefully stick a pair of chocolate wings onto each biscuit using melted chocolate.

To make the 15 flower biscuits: use melted chocolate to stick a chocolate flower onto each of the remaining undecorated Royals.

Colour the buttercream light-green and ice the cupcakes. Decorate cupcakes with some yellow sprinkles, then place a bee or flower biscuit in the centre of each.

Hot-air balloon

VANILLA CUSTARD CAKES

500 g softened butter

3 cups white sugar

6 eggs

1½ cups custard powder

4 cups self-raising flour

1 cup milk

3 teaspoons vanilla extract

METHOD

Preheat oven to 180°C. Grease one cup of a regular muffin pan, then grease and line a 20-cm round cake tin and two 16.5-cm round cake tins.

Cream butter and sugar until light and fluffy. Add eggs one at a time, beating well after each addition.

Gradually add sifted custard powder and flour and beat well. Beat in milk and vanilla extract until combined.

Pour a quarter of the batter into each of the small round cake tins, then divide the remaining half of the mixture into one muffin cup and the large round cake tin. Bake the muffin for 20 minutes, the small round cakes for 30 minutes and the large round cake for 45 minutes, or until a skewer inserted comes out clean.

Turn out and cool on wire racks.

continued

DECORATION

1 × 500-g packet white fondant

food colouring: blue, yellow, red, lime-green, brown, green

1-cm flower cutter

sheep, horse and cow biscuit cutters

10-cm polystyrene ball

1 × 500-g packet chocolate fondant

2 small round vanilla custard cakes (page 65)

1 large round vanilla custard cake (page 65)

1 vanilla custard muffin (page 65)

1 quantity basic icing (page 15)

1 quantity mock cream (page 16)

basket-weave piping tip

bamboo skewers

7-mm star piping tip

6-mm round piping tip

lollies: sour strawberry spaghetti

ASSEMBLY

Take a peach-sized piece of white fondant and divide in half; colour one portion blue and the other yellow. Make sandbags out of the yellow fondant by rolling four 2-cm balls and then moulding them into a teardrop shape. Roll out the blue fondant to 3 mm in thickness and cut out 30 flowers using the flower cutter. Set aside to dry.

Divide remaining white fondant into two portions (reserving a walnut-sized piece for later use). Roll out one portion to 5 mm in thickness and cut out four sheep with the biscuit cutter. Colour the second portion of fondant red; roll out to 5 mm in thickness and use to cover the polystyrene ball. Mould the edges of the fondant together at the base, adding more fondant if necessary, to make a balloon shape that tapers to a point. Place in a small bowl to dry.

Roll out the packet of chocolate fondant to 5 mm in thickness. Use the cutter to cut out four cows, then cut 15 strips about 1 cm wide and 5 cm long for the fence. Add the reserved white fondant to the remaining chocolate fondant and blend roughly. Roll out to 5 mm in thickness and cut out four horses.

Level the top of each vanilla custard cake and the muffin, then crumb coat each with basic icing. Leave to set.

Colour half of the mock cream lime-green. Divide the remaining mock cream into four portions. Leave one portion plain and colour each of the others a different colour: blue, brown and grass-green.

continued

Join the two small round cakes together with lime mock cream, then ice this cake and the large round cake all over with lime mock cream. Leave to set.

Ice the top half of the smaller lime cake with blue mock cream. Place the larger cake onto a cake board and then put the smaller cake on top.

Ice the top of the muffin with brown mock cream. Put the remaining brown mock cream into a piping bag fitted with the basket-weave tip and pipe a basket-weave pattern around the sides of the muffin (see technique on page 7). Carefully place the basket on top of the cake and push a bamboo skewer down through the centre of all three cakes to secure.

Use some mock cream to stick the animals around the sides of the round cakes; alternating between cows, sheep and horses.

Use a little mock cream to secure the fence onto the sides of the bottom cake. To make the grass: place the green mock cream into a piping bag with star tip attached and pipe a strip of mock cream around the bottom and top edges of the large cake (as shown in the photograph). Stick fondant flowers onto the grass. Use a little mock cream to stick the sandbags onto the basket.

Put white mock cream into a piping bag with round tip attached. Pipe clouds around the top edge of the smaller cake (see technique on page 6).

Insert a skewer 8 cm into the bottom of the red balloon and gently press it onto the basket on top of the cake. Carefully drape two pieces of strawberry spaghetti over the balloon (as shown), and secure the ends to the basket with a little brown mock cream.

Giraffe

CHOCOLATE CAKES

220 g butter

2 cups milk

3 cups self-raising flour

1 cup cocoa

2 cups white sugar

3 eggs

1 teaspoon vanilla extract

METHOD

Preheat oven to 180°C. Lightly grease and line two 23-cm square cake tins.

Gently heat butter and milk in a saucepan until butter is melted. Set aside.

Sift flour and cocoa into a large bowl. Add sugar, eggs and vanilla extract and beat until well combined. Gradually add milk mixture, beating until thick and smooth.

Divide batter into prepared cake tins and bake for 45 minutes, or until a skewer inserted into the centre comes out clean.

Turn out and cool on wire racks.

continued

ASSEMBLY

Level the tops of the two chocolate cakes, then use the templates provided to cut the required shapes from the cakes. Arrange the cake pieces on a cake board and join together with buttercream icing. Crumb coat the entire giraffe with basic icing. Leave to set.

Colour remaining buttercream yellow and use to ice the cake. Then colour the remaining yellow buttercream with orange colouring and place into a piping bag. Set aside.

Use scissors to cut out about ten 2-cm rounds from the orange sour straps. Arrange the orange spots over the giraffe's body, then pipe a swirl of orange icing onto each spot (as shown in the photograph).

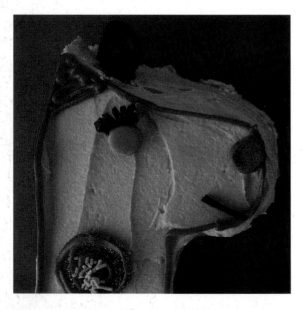

Pipe an outline of orange icing around the edge of the cake. Sprinkle each orange spot with yellow sprinkles.

Stick on a Smartie for the nose, one for the eye and three Smarties on each foot for toes (as shown). Cut six short matchsticks from the liquorice stick for the eyelashes, and a slightly longer one for the mouth. Stick onto the giraffe. Lastly, cut the chocolate bullet in half and stick onto the top of the head for the horns.

Ruby rose handbag

One day before: bake cake and assemble
On the day: apply finishing touches

VANILLA CUSTARD LOAF CAKES

500 g softened butter

3 cups white sugar

6 eggs

1½ cups custard powder

4 cups self-raising flour

1 cup milk

3 teaspoons vanilla extract

METHOD

Preheat oven to 180°C. Lightly grease and line two 25-cm × 11.5-cm loaf tins.

Cream butter and sugar until light and fluffy. Add eggs one at a time, beating well after each addition.

Gradually add sifted custard powder and flour and beat well. Beat in milk and vanilla extract until combined.

Pour batter into prepared tins and bake for 45 minutes, or until a skewer inserted into the centre of the cakes comes out clean.

Turn out and cool on a wire rack.

continued

DECORATION

2 vanilla custard loaf cakes
(page 73)

templates (page 210)

½ quantity basic icing (page 15)

1 × 500-g packet white fondant

food colouring: pink

½ quantity royal icing (page 17)

metal purse clasp (available
from craft stores)

non-toxic pastel colour: pink

fine paintbrush

pearl dust

plastic necklace

ASSEMBLY

Use the templates provided to cut the handbag shapes from the cakes. Use basic icing to join the small cake piece to the top of the larger cake piece. Round the edges with a sharp knife. Crumb coat the whole cake with basic icing.

Colour the fondant pink and roll out to 6 mm in thickness. Use to cover the entire cake, gathering the fondant at the base (as shown in the photograph) and securing with basic icing. Carefully place the handbag onto a cake board.

Colour the royal icing pink and place it into a piping bag. Cover the rose template provided with baking paper and practise tracing the design with icing. Once you are confident, pipe roses all over the cake.

Position the open purse clasp on top of the cake, being careful not to tear the fondant. Leave cake to dry overnight.

Scrape some powder from the pink-coloured pastel into a dish, then use a fine brush to apply the dust to the gathers and creases of the bag and to each rose. Leave to dry. Use the paintbrush to carefully dust the bag all over with pearl dust.

Drape the necklace over the bag.

Teddy bear's picnic

One day before: make royal icing and fondant decorations
On the day: bake cake and assemble

continued

VANILLA CUSTARD CAKE

250 g softened butter

1½ cups white sugar

3 eggs

¾ cup custard powder

2 cups self-raising flour

½ cup milk

2 teaspoons vanilla extract

METHOD

Preheat oven to 180°C. Grease and line a 20-cm round cake tin.

Cream butter and sugar until light and fluffy. Add eggs one at a time, beating well after each addition.

Gradually add sifted custard powder and flour and beat well. Beat in milk and vanilla extract until combined.

Pour batter into prepared tin and bake for 45 minutes, or until a skewer inserted into the centre of the cake comes out clean.

Turn out and cool on a wire rack.

1 quantity royal icing (page 17)

food colouring: lime-green, green, blue, black, red, brown, pink, orange

templates (page 211)

1 × 500-g packet white fondant

2-cm leaf cutter

fine paintbrush

assorted small flower cutters

knitting needle with rounded end

1-cm round piping tip

1 × 500-g packet chocolate fondant

7.5-cm polystyrene ball

1 round vanilla custard cake (page 75)

1 quantity mock cream (page 16)

bamboo skewer

toothpicks

ASSEMBLY

Divide the royal icing into six small bowls. Colour each portion a different colour: lime-green, green, blue, black, red and brown. Put each colour into a separate piping bag.

Using the templates provided, pipe the coloured royal icing to outline eight tree trunks, ten clumps of grass and 24 leaves. When outlines are dry, fill in with more icing (see fill-in technique on page 6).

Take a peach-sized piece of the white fondant and roll out to 5 mm in thickness. Cut out a 15-cm square for the picnic rug. Pipe the tartan pattern onto the rug (see technique on page 5) using the blue and red royal icing.

Divide the remaining white fondant into six pieces. Leave one portion plain and colour each of the others a different colour: blue, green, light-brown, pink and orange.

Roll out the green fondant to 5 mm in thickness and use the cutter to cut out 20 leaves. Draw veins on each leaf with the pointed end of a fine paintbrush. Use your fingers to shape each leaf.

Roll out the orange, pink, blue and remaining white fondant to 5 mm in thickness and use assorted cutters to cut out flowers. Gently push the rounded end of the knitting needle into the centre of each flower to shape it. Place flowers into an empty egg carton to dry – this helps them keep their shape.

continued

Use the round piping tip to cut out two 1-cm rounds from the pink fondant for the insides of the bear's ears. Colour a peanut-sized piece of white fondant red; roll it into a ball to make the bear's nose.

Roll out the chocolate fondant to 6 mm in thickness and cover the polystyrene ball, securing with royal icing. This will be the body. Flatten the bottom slightly and place in a small bowl to dry.

Using some of the leftover chocolate fondant, roll a ball about the half the size of the bear's body to make the head. Then make four sausages from the chocolate fondant, each measuring 4 cm long and 2 cm wide, for the bear's arms and legs. Flatten the end of each piece where the limb joins the body, and round the other end.

Cut two 2-cm rounds from the rolled chocolate fondant for ears. Use royal icing to stick a pink round of fondant onto each ear. Roll out the light-brown fondant and cut out four 15-mm rounds for the paws, a 3-cm round for the snout and a 5-cm round for the tummy. Stick each onto the bear with royal icing. Leave all fondant and royal icing decorations to dry overnight. (Store leftover royal icing in the fridge for later use.)

Cut the vanilla custard cake in half horizontally. Colour the mock cream green and use it to fill and ice the cake. Set aside to dry.

Carefully place the tartan picnic rug in the centre of the cake.

Poke a skewer through the bear's body from the top to the bottom, leaving 2 cm sticking out the top and the pointy end sticking out the bottom. Push the body onto the cake, in the centre of the rug. Dab some royal icing onto the base of the head, then gently push into position on the body. Use royal icing to attach the limbs to the body.

Stick the red fondant nose onto the snout with royal icing. Use white royal icing to pipe the eyes and brown to pipe the mouth (as shown in the photograph). Use black royal icing to pipe the detail onto each paw, to dot pupils onto the eyes and to draw on some eyelashes.

Using the photograph as a guide, stick all the fondant and royal icing decorations onto the cake and bear with royal icing.

Bunch of balloons

 One day before: make fondant decorations
On the day: bake cakes and assemble

VANILLA CUSTARD CAKES

500 g softened butter

3 cups white sugar

6 eggs

1½ cups custard powder

4 cups self-raising flour

1 cup milk

3 teaspoons vanilla extract

METHOD

Preheat oven to 180°C. Grease and line two 20-cm round cake tins.

Cream butter and sugar until light and fluffy. Add eggs one at a time, beating well after each addition.

Gradually add sifted custard powder and flour and beat well. Beat in milk and vanilla extract until combined.

Pour batter into prepared tins and bake for 45 minutes, or until a skewer inserted into the centre comes out clean.

Turn out and cool on wire racks.

continued

2 × 500-g packets white fondant

food colouring: yellow, purple, pink, light-blue, blue, red, lime-green, orange, green

2 round vanilla custard cakes (page 79)

1 quantity basic icing (page 15)

1 quantity mock cream (page 16)

5-mm round piping tip

number candle

ASSEMBLY

Divide the fondant into nine even portions and colour each a different colour: yellow, purple, pink, light-blue, blue, red, lime-green, orange and green. Make two balloons from each coloured fondant by rolling tablespoonfuls into balls.

Roll out half of each colour from the remaining fondant and cut long 4-mm wide strips to make flat streamers. With the remainder of the coloured fondant, roll long snakes 4 mm in diameter to make cylindrical streamers. Cut the flat and cylindrical streamers to varying lengths between 15 cm and 25 cm. Wrap each one around a pencil to make it curl, then set aside all fondant decorations to dry overnight.

Level each vanilla custard cake, then trim around the edge of one of the cakes until it is 12 cm in diameter. Crumb coat each cake with basic icing and leave to set.

Divide the mock cream into one medium bowl and one small bowl. Colour the larger portion blue and the other portion yellow.

Ice the small cake with yellow mock cream and the larger cake with blue mock cream (reserving a little of each colour for piping later on). Leave to dry, then place the blue cake onto a cake board and place the yellow cake on top of the blue cake.

continued

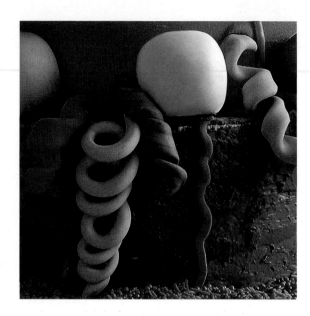

Stick a toothpick into the base of each balloon, leaving half the toothpick sticking out. Then press the balloons into the top of each cake (as shown in the photograph). Carefully position the streamers over the cake.

Put reserved yellow and blue mock cream into separate piping bags. Pipe 'strings' coming down from the base of each balloon (as shown).

Finally, place the number candle on top of the cake.

Train

One day before: make fondant parts
On the day: bake cake, assemble fondant decorations, ice and assemble cake

MARBLE CAKE

250 g softened butter

1½ cups white sugar

3 eggs

¾ cup custard powder

2 cups self-raising flour

½ cup milk

2 teaspoons vanilla extract

2 tablespoons cocoa

1 teaspoon strawberry essence

food colouring: red

METHOD

Preheat oven to 180°C. Grease and line a 23-cm square cake tin.

Cream butter and sugar until light and fluffy. Add eggs, one at a time, beating well after each addition.

Gradually add sifted custard powder and flour to egg mixture, mixing well. Beat in milk and vanilla extract.

Divide batter into three bowls. Leave one portion plain. To the second portion add sifted cocoa and mix, adding a little more milk if needed. To the third portion add strawberry essence and red food colouring. Mix well.

Drop spoonfuls of batter into the prepared cake tin, alternating between the three colours. Drag a knife through the batter to swirl the colours together. (See technique on page 2.)

Bake for 40 minutes, or until a skewer inserted into the centre of the cake comes out clean.

Turn out and cool on a wire rack.

continued

2 × 500-g packets white
fondant

food colouring: light-blue, red,
blue, orange, brown, green,
lime-green, yellow

templates (page 212)

1 square marble cake (page 83)

1 quantity basic icing (page 15)

lemon essence

fine paintbrush

½ quantity royal icing (page 17)

edible fine black marker pen

1 quantity buttercream icing
(page 13)

lollies: 1 packet Fads lollies,
liquorice straps, packet
Wonka Nerds, assorted small
lollies (e.g. bullets, jellybeans,
Smarties)

ASSEMBLY

Colour a marble-sized piece of white fondant light-blue.
Reserve a walnut-sized piece of white fondant for the
signs, then divide the remainder of the two packets of
fondant into seven portions. Colour each portion a
different colour: red, blue, orange, brown, green,
lime-green and yellow.

Roll out the lime-green fondant to 5 mm in thickness.
Using the template provided, cut out six base shapes.
Then use the templates as a guide to shape the engine
out of fondant: shape the body and cabin out of blue,
the windows and bumper bar out of red and the light
out of yellow. Make the engine roof out of light-blue,
then roll a 1-cm ball for the large chimney and a slightly
smaller ball for the little chimney. Use royal icing to stick
the engine pieces together (as shown in the photograph).
Set aside.

Roll out the remaining red, blue, orange, green and
yellow fondant to 5 mm in thickness. Using the templates
provided, cut out two carriage side walls and two
carriage end walls from each colour. Use the back of
a knife to draw horizontal lines on each wall. Lay flat
all the pieces on a sheet of baking paper to dry.

Roll out the reserved white fondant and use the template
provided to cut out six sign shapes. Roll out the brown
fondant to 5 mm in thickness and use the template to cut
out 24 wheels. Then cut a dozen 1-cm wide × 5-cm long
strips for wooden sleepers. Leave all fondant pieces to
dry overnight.

continued

Level the top of the marble cake and cut in half horizontally. Crumb coat each piece with basic icing. Leave to set.

Mix some brown paste food colouring with a little lemon essence and use to paint six Fads lollies for the signposts. Use the black pen to write a message on each sign (for example: 'Happy Birthday!', 'Party this way!'). Use royal icing to stick each sign onto one end of a Fads lolly.

Assemble the fondant carriage pieces: with royal icing, stick the pieces for each carriage onto a lime-green base piece, and four wheels onto the engine and each carriage. Leave to dry.

Colour the buttercream green. Place the two cake pieces end to end on a cake board and join with green buttercream. Ice the whole cake with buttercream and leave to set.

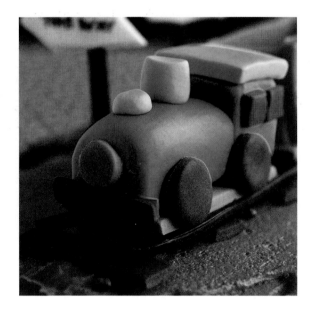

Lay the brown wooden sleepers in a row along the length of the cake, spaced about 2 cm apart. Cut two long strips from the liquorice straps for the metal train tracks, and place them lengthways over the sleepers (as shown in the photograph). Sprinkle some Wonka Nerds between the sleepers for gravel.

Position the engine onto the tracks at the left-hand end of the cake, then place the carriages along the track behind it, with an even amount of space between each.

Fill each carriage with assorted lollies. Finally, push the signposts into the cake behind the train.

Coat of arms

VANILLA CUSTARD CAKE

250 g softened butter

1½ cups white sugar

3 eggs

¾ cup custard powder

2 cups self-raising flour

½ cup milk

2 teaspoons vanilla extract

METHOD

Preheat oven to 180°C. Grease and line a 23-cm square cake tin.

Cream butter and sugar until light and fluffy. Add eggs one at a time, beating well after each addition.

Gradually add sifted custard powder and flour and beat well. Beat in milk and vanilla extract until combined.

Pour batter into prepared tin and bake for 40 minutes, or until a skewer inserted into the centre of the cake comes out clean.

Turn out and cool on a wire rack.

continued

DECORATION

1 square vanilla custard cake
  (page 87)

templates (page 213)

1 quantity basic icing (page 15)

2 × 500-g packets white
  fondant

food colouring: blue, red

5-cm star biscuit cutter

Play-Doh alphabet biscuit
  cutters

ASSEMBLY

This cake can be customised for whoever you are making it, simply by using the child's favourite colours and adding symbols of special relevance to that child.

Level the vanilla custard cake, then use the template provided to cut the shield shape from the cake. Crumb coat with basic icing and place onto a cake board.

Colour one packet of white fondant blue. Reserve a walnut-sized piece for use later, then roll out the remainder to 5 mm in thickness. Use to cover the cake.

Divide the second packet of fondant into two pieces. Leave one portion plain and colour the other portion red. Roll out each piece to 5 mm in thickness.

Use the templates provided to cut the two quarter pieces from the red fondant. Use some royal icing to stick them onto the cake (as shown in the photograph).

Use the template provided to cut a lion's head from the white fondant and use the star cutter to cut out a star. Brush the back of each with a little water and stick onto the blue sections of the cake.

With remaining white fondant, roll a 5-mm wide snake long enough to edge the top of the cake (as shown in the photograph). Secure with basic icing.

Roll out reserved blue fondant and cut out the child's initials using the alphabet cutters. Brush the back of each with water and stick onto the red sections of the cake.

Butterfly

CHOCOLATE CAKES

220 g butter

2 cups milk

3 cups self-raising flour

1 cup cocoa

2 cups white sugar

3 eggs

1 teaspoon vanilla extract

METHOD

Preheat oven to 180°C. Lightly grease and line two 23-cm square cake tins.

Gently heat butter and milk in a saucepan until butter is melted. Set aside.

Sift flour and cocoa into a large bowl. Add sugar, eggs and vanilla extract and beat until well combined. Gradually add milk mixture, beating until thick and smooth.

Divide batter into prepared cake tins and bake for 45 minutes, or until a skewer inserted into the centre comes out clean.

Turn out and cool on wire racks.

continued

DECORATION

2 square chocolate cakes
(page 91)

templates (pages 214–15)

2 quantities buttercream icing
(page 13)

1 quantity basic icing (page 15)

200 g unsalted butter

200 g dark cooking chocolate,
chopped

lollies: 1 liquorice strap

food colouring: red, yellow,
lime-green, blue, aqua, black

ASSEMBLY

Level the tops of the two chocolate cakes, then use the templates provided to cut the required shapes from the cakes. Arrange the two body pieces and the head piece on a cake board and join together with buttercream icing. Crumb coat each of the wing pieces with basic icing and set aside to dry.

Melt the butter in a small saucepan. Remove from heat and add chocolate, stirring until melted and smooth. Coat the body and head of the butterfly with melted chocolate. Cut two strips from the liquorice strap for antennae, and insert into the head.

Place 3 tablespoons of buttercream into each of three small bowls, and colour each portion a different colour: red, yellow and lime-green. Place into separate piping bags.

Divide the remaining buttercream into four medium bowls and colour each portion a different colour: lime-green, dark-blue, aqua and grey. Place the grey icing into a piping bag.

Starting at the tips of the wings (furthest from the body), ice a third of each wing piece with dark-blue buttercream, as well as the sides of the wings. Ice the centre third of each wing piece with aqua buttercream and ice the remaining third with lime-green.

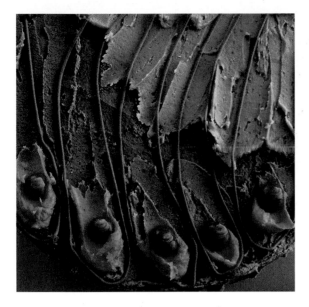

Using the lime, red and yellow buttercream, pipe dots around the edge of the wing pieces (as shown in the photograph).

Using the grey icing, pipe a thin outline around each wing piece and then pipe lines between the coloured dots (as shown).

Leave to set, then arrange the wings on either side of the body on the cake board.

Hot rocket

**VANILLA CUSTARD
LOAF CAKE**

250 g softened butter

1½ cups white sugar

3 eggs

¾ cup custard powder

2 cups self-raising flour

½ cup milk

2 teaspoons vanilla extract

METHOD

Preheat oven to 180°C. Lightly grease and line a
25-cm × 11.5-cm loaf tin.

Cream butter and sugar until light and fluffy. Add eggs
one at a time, beating well after each addition.

Gradually add sifted custard powder and flour and beat
well. Beat in milk and vanilla extract until combined.

Pour batter into prepared tin and bake for 45 minutes,
or until a skewer inserted into the centre of the cake
comes out clean.

Turn out and cool on a wire rack.

continued

ASSEMBLY

Trim one end of the vanilla custard loaf cake to level it, then place cake cut-side down. Starting from the top of the cake, use a bread knife to carve the cake into a four-sided bullet shape tapered to a point at the top.

Crumb coat the whole cake with basic icing and leave to set. Once set, secure the base of the cake to a cake board using buttercream. Ice the cake all over with buttercream.

Cut long thin strips from the liquorice straps. Place two of the strips over the cake (as shown in the photograph), and place one around the base of the cake.

Divide remaining buttercream into three bowls and colour each portion a different colour: red, orange and yellow. Place into separate piping bags.

Pipe four red stars around the point of the rocket, then pipe red flames coming up from the base (as shown in the photograph). Pipe smaller orange flames over the top of the red flames, then even smaller yellow flames over those.

To make the rocket's fins, round one top corner of each ice-cream wafer and then use the biscuit cutter to cut the round shape from the opposite bottom corner. Use basic icing to stick a thin liquorice strip onto the outside rounded edge of each wafer. Leave to dry, then push the wafers into the sides of the rocket (as shown in the photograph).

Building blocks

VANILLA CUSTARD LOAF CAKES

500 g softened butter

3 cups white sugar

6 eggs

1½ cups custard powder

4 cups self-raising flour

1 cup milk

3 teaspoons vanilla extract

METHOD

Preheat oven to 180°C. Lightly grease and line two 25-cm × 11.5-cm loaf tins.

Cream butter and sugar until light and fluffy. Add eggs one at a time, beating well after each addition.

Gradually add sifted custard powder and flour and beat well. Beat in milk and vanilla extract until combined.

Pour batter into prepared tins and bake for 45 minutes, or until a skewer inserted into the centre comes out clean.

Turn out and cool on wire racks.

continued

DECORATION

2 vanilla custard loaf cakes (page 97)

1 quantity basic icing (page 15)

3 × 500-g packets white fondant

food colouring: pink, blue, green

Play-Doh alphabet, number and star biscuit cutters

ASSEMBLY

Cut two even squares from each loaf cake. Crumb coat three of the squares with basic icing (freeze the last one for later use).

Take a walnut-sized ball of fondant from each packet; combine them and then colour pink. Leaving one packet of fondant plain, colour one packet blue and the other green. Roll out each of the three colours and the white fondant to 7 mm in thickness.

Cover one square of cake with white fondant, one with blue and one with green, securing with extra basic icing if needed. Using the Play-Doh cutters, cut out the letters a, b and c; the numbers 1, 2 and 3; and some stars from remaining rolled fondant. There should be 15 shapes in total, some in white and some in each of the other three colours.

Brush a little water onto the back of each letter and number and stick one onto each side and the tops of the cubes.

Position the blocks on a cake board, using toothpicks to secure in place if necessary.

Rocking horse

CHOCOLATE CAKES

220 g butter

2 cups milk

3 cups self-raising flour

1 cup cocoa

2 cups white sugar

3 eggs

1 teaspoon vanilla extract

METHOD

Preheat oven to 180°C. Lightly grease and line two 23-cm square cake tins.

Gently heat butter and milk in a saucepan until butter is melted. Set aside.

Sift flour and cocoa into a large bowl. Add sugar, eggs and vanilla extract and beat until well combined. Gradually add milk mixture, beating until thick and smooth.

Divide batter into prepared cake tins and bake for 45 minutes, or until a skewer inserted into the centre comes out clean.

Turn out and cool on wire racks.

continued

DECORATION

2 square chocolate cakes
(page 101)

templates (pages 216–17)

1 quantity buttercream icing
(page 13)

1 quantity basic icing (page 15)

**food colouring: red, cream,
brown, blue**

½ quantity royal icing (page 17)

silver cachous

lollies: 1 Smartie

ASSEMBLY

Level the tops of each chocolate cake, then use the templates provided to cut the required shapes from the cakes. Arrange the pieces on a cake board so that the corresponding letters on the template match up (A to A etc.) and join together with buttercream icing. Crumb coat the whole cake with basic icing, then leave to set.

Divide the remaining buttercream into two bowls and colour one portion red and the other cream. Divide the royal icing into two bowls and colour one portion brown and the other blue, then place each into a separate piping bag.

Ice the rocking horse's body with cream buttercream and then ice the rocker with red buttercream. Leave to set, then ice the saddle in red (as shown in the photograph). Use the blue and brown royal icing to pipe outlines and decorations onto the rocking horse (as shown).

Decorate the cake with silver cachous (as shown) and place a Smartie onto the head for the eye.

Spotty cake

VANILLA CUSTARD CAKES

500 g softened butter

3 cups white sugar

6 eggs

1½ cups custard powder

4 cups self-raising flour

1 cup milk

3 teaspoons vanilla extract

METHOD

Preheat oven to 180°C. Grease and line two 20-cm round cake tins.

Cream butter and sugar until light and fluffy. Add eggs one at a time, beating well after each addition.

Gradually add sifted custard powder and flour and beat well. Beat in milk and vanilla extract until combined.

Pour batter into prepared tins and bake for 45 minutes, or until a skewer inserted into the centre comes out clean.

Turn out and cool on wire racks.

continued

ASSEMBLY

Level off the top of the two vanilla custard cakes, then crumb coat each with basic icing. Leave to set.

Whip the thickened cream until soft peaks form, sweeten with icing sugar to taste. Sandwich the cakes together with the whipped cream.

Colour the mock cream with aqua food colouring, then ice the cake all over.

Place a sheet of baking paper over the button templates provided. Use a teaspoon to carefully place coloured sprinkles into each circle. Reserve about ten white chocolate buttons for decorating, then put the remainder into a microwave-safe bowl and heat on MEDIUM for 20 seconds at a time, stirring between bursts, until melted and smooth. Drop a small spoonful of melted chocolate onto each pile of sprinkles, to make sprinkle chocolate buttons. Leave to set.

Arrange the sprinkle buttons and reserved plain white buttons all over the cake. Place candles on top of the cake.

Fire truck

VANILLA CUSTARD LOAF CAKES

500 g softened butter

3 cups white sugar

6 eggs

1½ cups custard powder

4 cups self-raising flour

1 cup milk

3 teaspoons vanilla extract

METHOD

Preheat oven to 180°C. Lightly grease and line two 25-cm × 11.5-cm loaf tins.

Cream butter and sugar until light and fluffy. Add eggs one at a time, beating well after each addition.

Gradually add sifted custard powder and flour and beat well. Beat in milk and vanilla extract until combined.

Pour batter into prepared tins and bake for 45 minutes, or until a skewer inserted into the centre comes out clean.

Turn out and cool on wire racks.

continued

ASSEMBLY

Cut a 10-cm square block from the first loaf cake.
This will be the cabin. Then cut two more pieces from
the remainder of this cake, each measuring 5 cm high ×
6 cm wide × 13 cm long. These pieces will make the base
for the truck to rest on. From the second loaf cake, cut
out a rectangle 7 cm high × 10 cm wide × 18 cm long.
This will be the back of the truck. (Freeze the rest of this
cake for later use.) Crumb coat each of the cake shapes
with basic icing and leave to set.

Roll out the first packet of white fondant to 7 mm in
thickness. Use to cover the cabin cake piece, securing
with basic icing. Trim off excess. Cut some 15-mm wide
strips from the remaining rolled fondant for the sides
and rear of the truck (as shown in the photograph).
Use the templates provided to cut out the mudguards
and headlights.

Colour the remainder of the first packet of fondant
cream and roll out six cylindrical hoses that are each
1 cm in diameter and 2 cm shorter than the length
of the back of the truck.

Colour the leftover cream fondant black. Roll out to
7 mm in thickness, then use the templates provided to
cut out the windscreen, side windows, bull bar and two
rear mudguards. Use basic icing to stick the windows
onto the cabin.

Colour the second packet of fondant red. Roll out and use to cover the sides and rear of the back of the truck, securing with basic icing. Trim off any excess. Cut a red strip to cover the bottom half of the cabin (as shown in the photograph) and secure with basic icing. Use basic icing to stick the white fondant strips along the sides and rear of the truck.

Place the two base-cake pieces end to end on a cake board and join with royal icing. Divide the remaining royal icing into two bowls; colour one portion red and the other portion grey. Use the grey icing to ice the base piece of cake. Leave to set. Colour the remaining grey icing black and place it and the red icing into separate piping bags.

For the wheels, pipe a black outline around the edge of each Mint Slice biscuit, and then pipe four dots in the centre of each (as shown in the photograph). Leave to set. When icing has dried, use basic icing to stick the mudguards to the back and front wheels.

Use icing to stick the wheels on either side of the base cake piece, towards the front and back. Position the cabin and back of the truck onto the grey base cake and secure with skewers, pushing two through from the cabin into the back of the truck.

Using the black icing, pipe outlines and details around the truck, and pipe the word FIRE onto the side of the truck, towards the back (as shown). Then use the red icing to pipe diagonal stripes along the white strip that runs along the sides and rear of the truck.

Use icing to stick on the headlights. Cut four small squares from an orange wildberry for the indicators, and four from a red wildberry for brake lights. Stick on to the front and back of the truck (as shown). Cut two more orange wildberries and two red wildberries in half horizontally. Use basic icing to stick a red berry top onto an orange berry bottom, to make the lights. Stick these onto the top of the cabin.

Place the hoses on the back of the truck (as shown).

Castle in the clouds

VANILLA CUSTARD CAKES

500 g softened butter

3 cups white sugar

6 eggs

1½ cups custard powder

4 cups self-raising flour

1 cup milk

3 teaspoons vanilla extract

METHOD

Preheat oven to 180°C. Lightly grease and line two 23-cm square cake tins.

Cream butter and sugar until light and fluffy. Add eggs one at a time, beating well after each addition.

Gradually add sifted custard powder and flour and beat well. Beat in milk and vanilla extract until combined.

Divide batter into prepared cake tins and bake for 40 minutes, or until a skewer inserted into the centre comes out clean.

Turn out and cool on wire racks.

continued

ASSEMBLY

Level the tops of the two vanilla custard cakes. Leave one cake whole; this will be the bottom level. Use the templates provided to cut the required shapes from the second cake. Crumb coat each cake piece with basic icing, then join together the two top-level pieces with more icing to make a square.

Roll out the white fondant to 5 mm in thickness and cover each piece of cake, securing with basic icing.

Using the 'cone cover' template provided, cut a piece of rolled fondant to cover each ice-cream cone in and secure with basic icing.

Using the template provided, cut lots of long crenellations (edging strips) out of the fondant. Secure these edging strips to the sides of each of the three main square pieces of cake with basic icing. Place one of the covered ice-cream cones upside-down onto each of the five turrets (the smallest cake squares). Then use basic icing to secure edging strips around these cakes (as shown in the photograph).

Place the bottom-level cake piece onto a cake board, securing it to the board with a little basic icing on the underneath. Place the middle-level cake square on top of this, with the corners of the top cake pointing towards the straight edges of the bottom cake. Place the top-level cake square in the centre of the middle cake, with the edges parallel to the cake below.

Using basic icing, secure a covered cone to each corner of the bottom layer, then attach edging strips around the base of each cone. Stick one of the turrets (with cone attached) into each corner of the middle level. Place the remaining turret onto the top level of the castle.

Cut three flags from each length of ribbon and glue or tape each flag onto a toothpick. Carefully stick a flag into the top of each cone.

With a paintbrush, lightly brush pearl dust and lustre dust over the top of each cone and along the crenellations. Finally, arrange the Persian fairy floss on the cake board around the bottom of the cake.

What a mess!

🕐 **One day before:** prepare and ice cake, make buckets and fondant parts
On the day: assemble

INGREDIENTS

4 litres vanilla ice-cream

5 assorted chocolate bars

2 × 23-cm round cake tins

600 ml thickened cream

2 teaspoons icing sugar

floristry wire

4 corrugated paper espresso cups

1 × 500-g packet white fondant

food colouring: red, yellow, blue, green, brown, cream

½ × 395-g tin condensed milk

ASSEMBLY

Remove ice-cream from freezer and set aside to soften for 10 minutes. (Remember that when using ice-cream, it's important to work quickly and refreeze the ice-cream as soon as possible. If the ice-cream starts to melt, return to the freezer for a few minutes.)

Chop and crush chocolate bars, then mix into the softened ice-cream.

Line the two cake tins with cling wrap, leaving plenty of excess overhanging. Fill tins with softened ice-cream, pressing it into the tins with the back of a metal spoon. Fill until ice-cream is 1 cm from the top of each tin. Completely cover the top of the cake with the overhanging cling wrap. Return to the freezer for 2 hours.

Reserve ½ cup of the thickened cream, then add icing sugar to remaining cream and whip until stiff peaks form. Turn ice-cream cakes out of the tins; place onto a serving plate, one on top of the other, and gently press together. Quickly ice the cake with the sweetened whipped cream. Return to the freezer and freeze overnight.

continued

Cut four 8-cm lengths of floristry wire. Use a skewer to poke two holes, opposite each other, near the top of each espresso cup. For each cup, hook the end of a piece of wire through one hole, bending it over to stop it coming out. Then poke the other end of the wire through the opposite hole and secure, to make a handle for the 'bucket'.

Take three walnut-sized pieces from the white fondant and colour each of them brown. Shape each piece into a paintbrush handle: the main part measuring 1 cm high and 4 cm wide, and the handle itself 1 cm in diameter.

Colour another three walnut-sized pieces of fondant cream. Shape each into a 3-cm square that is 1 cm high. Using scissors, make 2-cm long cuts along one edge of each square, to make the brush's bristles. Use a little water to join one of these brush heads to each of the paintbrush handles. Leave to dry overnight.

Combine the condensed milk with reserved thickened cream in a medium-sized bowl. Whip together until thick, then divide into four small bowls. Colour each portion a different colour: red, yellow, blue and green. Fill each espresso-cup bucket with one of the coloured creams.

Remove cake from the freezer. Carefully position the espresso cups on top of the cake, letting the coloured cream run out over the cake (try to not let the colours mix). Dip the brush of each paintbrush into one of the coloured creams, then position the brushes on the cake.

Refreeze cake until ready to serve.

Crocodile

CHOCOLATE CAKES

220 g butter

2 cups milk

3 cups self-raising flour

1 cup cocoa

2 cups white sugar

3 eggs

1 teaspoon vanilla extract

METHOD

Preheat oven to 180°C. Lightly grease and line two 23-cm square cake tins.

Gently heat butter and milk in a saucepan until butter is melted. Set aside.

Sift flour and cocoa into a large bowl. Add sugar, eggs and vanilla extract and beat until well combined. Gradually add milk mixture, beating until thick and smooth.

Divide batter into prepared cake tins and bake for 45 minutes, or until a skewer inserted into the centre comes out clean.

Turn out and cool on wire racks.

continued

ASSEMBLY

Level the tops of the two chocolate cakes, then use the templates provided to cut the required shapes from the cakes. Crumb coat each piece with basic icing, reserving about four tablespoons for piping later. Leave to set.

Colour a third of the buttercream dark-green and use to ice a cake board. Arrange the cake pieces on the cake board so that the corresponding letters on the template match up (A to A etc.), and with the nose and head pieces positioned on the snout as shown by the placement lines. Join together with buttercream icing.

Colour remaining buttercream bright-green, and use to ice the whole cake.

Cut four slices from the liquorice stick for the pupils and nostrils. Cut one marshmallow in half horizontally for the whites of the eyes. Cut a thin slice from the second marshmallow and then cut the slice into small triangles for teeth.

Cut a liquorice strap into long thin strips, then cut the strips into eight short pieces for eyelashes, and two longer pieces for eyebrows.

Using basic icing, stick a yellow Smartie to each of the marshmallow halves. Allow to dry before sticking a round liquorice slice on top of each Smartie. When icing is dry, stick the eyes onto the head.

continued

Carefully arrange the liquorice eyebrows and eyelashes above the eyes. Stick on the liquorice nostrils and marshmallow teeth (as shown in the photograph).

Colour the reserved basic icing red and place into a piping bag. Using the photographs as a guide, pipe red icing to make the crocodile's scales, mouth and feet.

Happy birthday cupcakes

CHOCOLATE CUPCAKES

220 g butter

2 cups milk

3 cups self-raising flour

1 cup cocoa

2 cups white sugar

3 eggs

1 teaspoon vanilla extract

METHOD

Preheat oven to 180°C. Line three regular muffin pans with 30 cupcake papers.

Gently heat butter and milk in a saucepan until butter is melted. Set aside.

Sift flour and cocoa into a large bowl. Add sugar, eggs and vanilla extract and beat until well combined. Gradually add milk mixture, beating until thick and smooth.

Divide batter into cupcake papers and bake for 20 minutes, or until a skewer inserted into the centre of a cupcake comes out clean.

Turn out and cool on wire racks.

continued

HONEY SNAPS

125 g softened butter

⅓ cup castor sugar

1 teaspoon vanilla extract

⅔ cup plain flour

⅔ cup self-raising flour

½ teaspoon ground nutmeg

1 tablespoon honey

2 tablespoons milk

Play-Doh alphabet biscuit
  cutters

METHOD

Cream butter, sugar and vanilla extract until light and fluffy. Add sifted dry ingredients and mix to combine.

Soften the honey in the microwave for 10 seconds, then pour into batter. Beat in milk.

Turn dough onto a lightly floured board and knead gently. Cover dough with cling wrap and refrigerate for 30 minutes.

Preheat oven to 180°C. Grease or line baking trays.

Divide dough into three pieces. Roll out each portion between two sheets of cling wrap, to prevent sticking, until 5 mm in thickness.

Using the alphabet cutters, cut out letters to spell HAPPY BIRTHDAY and the child's name. Place onto prepared trays and bake for 6 minutes, or until golden.

Cool on a wire rack.

continued

DECORATION

1 quantity royal icing (honey consistency) (page 17)

food colouring: red, blue

honey snaps (page 122)

1 quantity buttercream icing (page 13)

30 chocolate cupcakes (page 121)

ASSEMBLY

Divide the royal icing into three bowls. Leave one portion plain, colour one red and the other blue. Place each portion into a separate piping bag.

Pipe around the edge of each cooled honey snap biscuit with one of the three coloured icings, then leave to dry. Once set, fill in the outlines with more icing. Set biscuits aside to dry.

Divide the buttercream icing into three bowls. Leave one portion plain, colour one red and colour the other blue. Ice cupcakes with the different coloured buttercreams. Position a letter biscuit upright in the centre of each cupcake.

Stack of presents

CHOCOLATE CAKES

220 g butter

2 cups milk

3 cups self-raising flour

1 cup cocoa

2 cups white sugar

3 eggs

1 teaspoon vanilla extract

METHOD

Preheat oven to 180°C. Lightly grease and line two 23-cm square cake tins.

Gently heat butter and milk in a saucepan until butter is melted. Set aside.

Sift flour and cocoa into a large bowl. Add sugar, eggs and vanilla extract and beat until well combined. Gradually add milk mixture, beating until thick and smooth.

Divide batter into prepared cake tins and bake for 45 minutes, or until a skewer inserted into the centre comes out clean.

Turn out and cool on wire racks.

continued

ASSEMBLY

Level the top of each chocolate cake. Leave the first cake
as it is; this will be the bottom present. Cut a 16-cm
square from the second cake; this will be the middle
present. From the remainder of the second cake, cut
out two rectangles measuring 10 cm × 4 cm. Use mock
cream to join these two pieces together, to create a
rectangle measuring 10 cm × 8 cm. This will be the top
present. Crumb coat each of the cakes with basic icing.

Colour one packet of white fondant blue. Roll out to
7 mm in thickness and use to cover the large square
cake, securing with mock cream. Place onto a cake
board.

Divide the second packet of white fondant into four
pieces. Leave one portion plain and colour each of
the others a different colour: red, pink and green.

Roll out the white fondant to 4 mm in thickness. Use
the 1-cm piping tip to cut out lots of rounds from the
fondant. Use some basic icing to stick them all over
the blue cake.

Roll out the red fondant to 5 mm in thickness and cut
two long strips, about 2 cm wide for ribbon. Brush with
water, then stick them onto the blue cake in a cross (as
shown in the photograph). Trim off any excess. Set aside.

Roll out the pink fondant to 5 mm in thickness, and use
to cover the rectangular cake, securing with a little basic
icing. Set aside.

continued

To make the ribbon and bow for the top present, roll out the green fondant to 5 mm in thickness and cut out two long strips that are 2 cm wide. Stick these onto the pink cake in a cross (as shown in the photograph). To make the bow, cut a strip of green fondant that is 2 cm wide and 20 cm long. Take each end of the strip and fold into the centre. Secure with a little royal icing. Cut another strip 2 cm wide and 5 cm long for the knot of the bow. Place this piece over the join on the first piece, tuck each end underneath and secure with icing. Cut two more strips measuring 2 cm wide and 10 cm long. Stick one end of each strip under the knot of the bow for the ribbon tails. Leave to dry.

Colour the remaining mock cream green and use it to ice the 16-cm square cake. Leave to set.

Divide the royal icing into five small bowls and colour each portion a different colour: pink, red, green, lime-green and black. Place into separate piping bags and cut a very small hole in the tip of each.

Cover the rose template provided with baking paper and practise tracing the outline with black royal icing. Once you're confident, pipe black roses over the top and sides of the green cake (leaving a space in the centre of the top, where the pink cake will sit). Leave to set for 20 minutes, then use the other icing colours to fill in the outline (using the photograph as a guide). Leave to set.

Place the green cake on top of the blue cake, then place the pink cake on top of the green cake. Carefully secure the fondant bow to the top present with a little basic icing.

Sailing boats

Two days before: bake and begin decorating spice biscuits
One day before: finish decorating spice biscuits
On the day: bake cake and assemble

BOAT SPICE BISCUITS

½ cup golden syrup

½ cup white sugar

125 g butter, chopped

2 cups plain flour

2 teaspoons ground cinnamon

1 teaspoon mixed spice

½ teaspoon ground cloves

1 teaspoon bicarbonate of soda

template (page 223)

METHOD

Preheat oven to 180°C. Grease baking trays.

Heat golden syrup and sugar in a medium saucepan. Bring to the boil, then remove from heat. Add butter and stir until melted.

Sift all dry ingredients into a large bowl. Add syrup and mix well. Cover bowl with cling wrap and refrigerate for 30 minutes.

Divide dough into four pieces. Roll out each portion between two sheets of cling wrap, to prevent sticking, until 5 mm in thickness.

Use the template provided to cut out three boat shapes from the dough, and place onto prepared trays. (If you have leftover dough, you can freeze it for later use, or bake in whatever shapes you desire then store in an airtight container for up to two weeks.)

Bake for 7 minutes, or until golden. Remove from the oven immediately and cool on a wire rack. Allow to cool completely before decorating.

continued

VANILLA CUSTARD CAKE

250 g softened butter

1½ cups white sugar

3 eggs

¾ cup custard powder

2 cups self-raising flour

½ cup milk

2 teaspoons vanilla extract

METHOD

Preheat oven to 180°C. Grease and line a 20-cm round cake tin.

Cream butter and sugar until light and fluffy. Add eggs one at a time, beating well after each addition.

Gradually add sifted custard powder and flour and beat well. Beat in milk and vanilla extract until combined.

Pour batter into prepared tin and bake for 45 minutes, or until a skewer inserted into the centre of the cake comes out clean.

Turn out and cool on a wire rack.

continued

ASSEMBLY

Divide the royal icing into five small bowls and colour each portion a different colour: black, red, blue, green and yellow. Place each colour into a separate piping bag. Pipe the sails, mast, hull and your child's age onto the cooled spice biscuits (as shown in the photograph). Leave to set overnight. (Store royal icing in the fridge.)

The next day, ice the other side of each biscuit. Leave to set overnight.

Level the top of the vanilla custard cake, then crumb coat the cake with basic icing. Leave to set, then place onto a cake board.

Colour most of the buttercream blue, reserving a small amount of white for the tips of the waves. Reserve a small amount of blue for assembling the cake, then use an offset palette knife to ice the cake with the remaining blue buttercream. Use the knife to create some 'waves' in the icing. Add a little of the white buttercream to the tips of the waves. Carefully apply yellow and orange sprinkles around the base of the cake for the sand (see technique on page 4).

Decorate the sides of the cake with fish lollies, and apple sour tubes for seaweed.

Apply some of the reserved blue buttercream to the bottom of each boat biscuit and position boats upright on top of the cake.

Pig in mud

One day before: prepare and ice cake, make fondant parts
On the day: assemble

INGREDIENTS

4 litres vanilla ice-cream

2 × 250-g packets chocolate-coated honeycomb

2 × 23-cm round cake tins

500 ml thickened cream

icing sugar, to taste

food colouring: green, pink, blue

200 g dark chocolate, chopped

1 × 500-g packet white fondant

8-mm round piping tip

7.5-cm polystyrene ball

½ quantity royal icing (page 17)

toothpicks

templates (page 224)

1 × 500-g packet chocolate fondant

lollies: 10 assorted lollies

ASSEMBLY

Take ice-cream out of the freezer and set aside to soften for about 10 minutes. (Remember that when using ice-cream, it's important to work quickly and refreeze the ice-cream as soon as possible. If the ice-cream starts to melt, return to the freezer for a few minutes.)

Leave the honeycomb in the packets and crush with a rolling pin. Mix crushed honeycomb pieces into the softened ice-cream.

Line the two cake tins with cling wrap, leaving plenty of excess overhanging. Fill with ice-cream, pressing into the tins with the back of a metal spoon. Fill until ice-cream is 1 cm from the top of each tin. Completely cover the top of each cake with the overhanging cling wrap. Return to the freezer for 2 hours.

Turn ice-cream cakes out of the tins. Place onto a serving plate, one on top of the other, and gently press together. Return to the freezer.

continued

Sweeten 300 ml of the thickened cream with icing sugar to taste, and colour with green food colouring. Whip until stiff peaks form, then use to ice the cake. Return cake to freezer.

To make chocolate ganache, bring remaining thickened cream to the boil in a heavy-based saucepan. Remove from heat and add dark chocolate. Stir until chocolate is melted and smooth. Set aside to cool until the chocolate mixture is beginning to harden but is still creamy in texture. Use ganache to ice the top of the cake, reserving a few tablespoons for later use. Return cake to freezer. Leave in freezer overnight.

Take a marble-sized piece of white fondant and roll out to 5 mm in thickness. Use the piping tip to cut out two rounds for eyes. Colour the remaining white fondant pink. Roll out and use to cover the polystyrene ball, securing with some royal icing. This will be the pig's body. Place in a small bowl to dry.

From the remaining pink fondant, roll a solid ball about the half the size of the pig's body for the head. Then roll five 2-cm balls for the feet and snout, pressing gently to flatten the top and bottom of each slightly. Roll a little sausage about 5 mm thick and 7 cm long for the tail. Shape tail into a tight curl, then poke a 3-cm long piece of toothpick into one end, leaving half sticking out. Make two ears, using the template provided as a guide.

Colour a walnut-sized piece of the pink fondant a darker shade of pink and roll tiny balls for the pads on the feet, the nostrils and belly button. Roll out remainder to 4 mm in thickness and use the template to cut out the insides of the ears. Press the little balls onto the feet, nose and body, and press the insides of the ears onto the ears (as shown in the photograph).

Roll out the chocolate fondant to 4 mm in thickness. For the fence, cut 20 strips about 1 cm wide, and cut these into uneven lengths, between 6 cm and 10 cm long.

Colour remaining pink fondant with brown colouring and mould into a rectangle 15 mm high × 2 cm wide × 7 cm long. This will be the trough. Leave all fondant decorations to dry overnight.

To put the pig together: use royal icing and toothpicks to secure the head to the body, and then use icing to attach the legs, ears, tail and snout. Use a little royal icing to stick on the eyes.

continued

Working quickly, place the pig onto the cake and use reserved ganache to stick the fence around the edge of the cake (as shown in the photograph on page 135). Place the trough next to the pig and use ganache to stick lollies onto the top of it.

Colour a teaspoon of royal icing blue and a teaspoon dark-pink. Place into separate piping bags and use the blue to pipe pupils onto the eyes, and the pink to pipe a mouth (as shown in the photograph below).

Return cake to freezer until ready to serve.

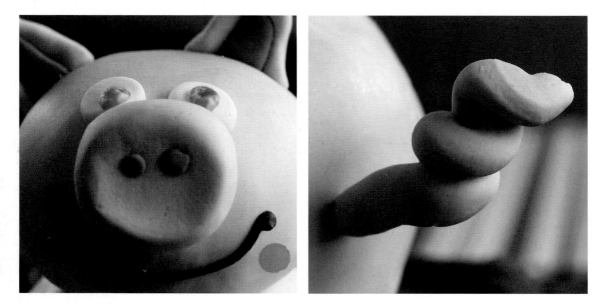

Tractor

VANILLA CUSTARD LOAF CAKES

500 g softened butter

3 cups white sugar

6 eggs

1½ cups custard powder

4 cups self-raising flour

1 cup milk

3 teaspoons vanilla extract

METHOD

Preheat oven to 180°C. Lightly grease and line two 25-cm × 11.5-cm loaf tins.

Cream butter and sugar until light and fluffy. Add eggs one at a time, beating well after each addition.

Gradually add sifted custard powder and flour and beat well. Beat in milk and vanilla extract until combined.

Divide batter into prepared loaf tins and bake for 45 minutes, or until a skewer inserted into the centre comes out clean.

Turn out and cool on wire racks.

continued

ASSEMBLY

Level the top of the first loaf cake and cut 6 cm off one end. From this small piece, shape a rectangle that is 2 cm high × 6 cm wide × 9 cm long . This will be the bonnet of the tractor. The remainder of this loaf cake will be the main body of the tractor. Crumb coat each piece with basic icing.

From the second loaf cake cut a rectangle that is 10 cm high and 9 cm wide for the cabin. Crumb coat this piece. Set aside the remainder of this cake for the wheels.

Use royal icing to stick the bonnet onto the top of the main body of the tractor (as shown in the photograph).

Use orange and yellow colouring to colour one packet of white fondant egg-yolk yellow. Roll out to 7 mm in thickness and use to cover the main body of the tractor and the bonnet, securing with royal icing. Place onto a cake board.

Take a walnut-sized piece from the second packet of white fondant and add black colouring to make it grey. Roll into a cylinder 13 cm long and 1 cm wide for the exhaust pipe. Carefully push a bamboo skewer into the pipe from one end, leaving a few centimetres sticking out the bottom. Set aside to dry.

Roll out the remaining white fondant to 7 mm in thickness and use it to cover the cabin piece, securing with royal icing. Place cabin onto the body of the tractor and secure with royal icing and toothpicks.

continued

From the remaining rolled yellow fondant, cut out a 9-cm square to exactly fit the roof of the cabin. Brush the back with a little water and stick onto the cabin roof.

Take the piece of cake set aside for the wheels and cut it into four even slices. Then use the 10-cm biscuit cutter to cut rounds from two of the slices for the back wheels and use the 8-cm biscuit cutter to cut rounds from the two remaining slices for the front wheels. Crumb coat each wheel with basic icing. Leave to set.

Place dark chocolate into a microwave-safe bowl and heat on MEDIUM for 20 seconds at a time, stirring in between bursts, until melted and smooth. Allow to cool until chocolate is the consistency of honey, then spread over the wheels. Leave to set.

Use a sharp knife to cut out two 9-cm rounds and two 7-cm rounds from the remaining rolled white fondant. Use icing to stick one of the larger rounds into the centre of each back wheel, and a smaller round into the centre of each front wheel. Use the round piping tip to cut out two 1-cm rounds from white fondant for headlights, then stick them onto the front of the tractor with royal icing. Cut 16 slices from the liquorice sticks, for the wheel nuts, and stick four of these rounds into the centre of each wheel (as shown). Leave to set.

Colour the remaining royal icing black and put into a piping bag. Pipe a thin black outline around the edges of the tractor, a grill onto the front and a windscreen wiper onto the front window (as shown in the photograph).

Push the exhaust into place on the body of the tractor (as shown). To position each wheel, stick a toothpick into the side of the tractor and carefully push the wheel on.

Giant cupcake

CHOCOLATE CAKES

220 g butter

2 cups milk

3 cups self-raising flour

1 cup cocoa

2 cups white sugar

3 eggs

1 teaspoon vanilla extract

METHOD

Preheat oven to 180°C. Grease a 20-cm brioche tin and a 16-cm pudding tin.

Gently heat butter and milk in a saucepan until butter is melted. Set aside.

Sift flour and cocoa into a large bowl. Add sugar, eggs and vanilla extract and beat until well combined. Gradually add milk mixture, beating until thick and smooth.

Divide batter into prepared tins. Bake the pudding cake for 35 minutes and the brioche cake for 40 minutes, or until a skewer inserted into the centre comes out clean.

Turn out and cool on wire racks.

continued

ASSEMBLY

Colour fondant with a little cream food colouring and roll out to 6 mm in thickness. Level the top of the chocolate brioche cake, then place cut-side down and crumb coat the sides with basic icing (step 1). Carefully cover the cake with the fondant, pressing it down into the indentations with the handle of a wooden spoon (step 2). Trim around the edges and remove excess. Turn cake onto its base and place on a cake board. Set aside.

Colour leftover fondant pink. Roll out to 3 mm in thickness and use the cutters to cut out about 14 small flowers and one large flower. Gently push the rounded end of the knitting needle into the centre of each small flower, to shape it.

Colour 3 tablespoons of basic icing green and put into a piping bag. Pipe a small blob of icing into the centre of each fondant flower. Set flowers aside to dry.

continued

Level the top of the pudding cake and place cut-side down. Round the top edges of the cake with a sharp knife. Crumb coat with basic icing and place cut-side down on top of the brioche cake (step 3).

Ice the pudding cake with the chocolate buttercream, making sure to fill in any gaps between the two cakes.

Position small fondant flowers around the edge of the cake, and place the large fondant flower on top. Scatter pink cachous over the top of the cake.

Footy boots

CHOCOLATE LOAF CAKES

220 g butter

2 cups milk

3 cups self-raising flour

1 cup cocoa

2 cups white sugar

3 eggs

1 teaspoon vanilla extract

METHOD

Preheat oven to 180°C. Lightly grease and line two 25-cm × 11.5-cm loaf tins.

Gently heat butter and milk in a saucepan until butter is melted. Set aside.

Sift flour and cocoa into a large bowl. Add sugar, eggs and vanilla extract and beat until well combined. Gradually add milk mixture, beating until thick and smooth.

Divide batter into prepared loaf tins and bake for 45 minutes, or until a skewer inserted into the centre comes out clean.

Turn out and cool on wire racks.

continued

2 chocolate loaf cakes
   (pages 145)

templates (page 224)

½ quantity basic icing (page 15)

3 × 500-g packets white
   fondant

food colouring: red, light-blue,
   blue, brown

5-cm round biscuit cutter

Play-Doh number biscuit
   cutters

2-mm round piping tip

toothpick

non-toxic pastel colour: black

very fine paintbrush

lollies: liquorice spaghetti

ASSEMBLY

Use the template provided to cut a boot shape from
each loaf cake. Round off the edges with a sharp knife
and crumb coat each with basic icing.

Take an egg-sized piece from the first packet of white
fondant and colour it red. Colour a third of the leftover
fondant light-blue, and the remainder dark-blue.

Roll out the dark-blue fondant to 5 mm in thickness.
To make the opening of the shoe, use the dark-blue
fondant to cover the top flat section of each boot,
securing with a little basic icing.

Roll out the second packet of white fondant and use the
template provided to cut out two tongues. Use basic
icing to stick one onto the front of each boot.

Combine all remaining white fondant and divide into two
even pieces. Roll out each portion to 7 mm in thickness,
and from each cut out a rectangle measuring about
30 cm × 45 cm. Use the round biscuit cutter to cut a hole
slightly to the left of centre on each piece. Drape one
piece over each shoe, positioning the hole over the
shoe opening, so the dark-blue fondant shows through.
Press the white fondant down to cover the whole shoe.
Cut away any excess and secure with basic icing.

Cut a slit from the opening down the centre of the front
of each shoe to open up the top, being careful not to cut
the tongue underneath.

continued

Roll out the light-blue fondant and cut out six strips 15 mm wide for each shoe. Stick onto the sides of the shoes with basic icing, trimming to length (as shown in the photograph). Using the templates provided, cut out the two heel and two toe pieces and stick onto the shoes (as shown).

Roll out the red fondant and use the Play-Doh cutter to cut out the number that corresponds to the child's age. Stick a number onto the side of each boot.

Using the piping tip, cut 12 holes for the shoelaces to thread through, six on each side of the front opening of each boot, and spaced about 15 mm apart.

Use a toothpick to dot around the edges of the blue and red fondant, to look like stitching. Scrape some powder from the black pastel colour into a dish and use the paintbrush to dust it over the stitching lines. Set the boots aside to dry for a few hours.

Gently push pieces of liquorice spaghetti into the holes to lace each boot (as shown).

Fairy's garden

 One day before: make fondant decorations
On the day: bake cake and assemble

CHOCOLATE CAKE

110 g butter

1 cup milk

1½ cups self-raising flour

½ cup cocoa

1 cup white sugar

2 eggs

½ teaspoon vanilla extract

METHOD

Preheat oven to 180°C. Grease and line a 20-cm round cake tin.

Gently heat butter and milk in a saucepan until butter is melted. Set aside.

Sift flour and cocoa into a large bowl. Add sugar, eggs and vanilla extract and beat until well combined. Gradually add milk mixture, beating until thick and smooth.

Pour batter into prepared tin and bake for 40 minutes, or until a skewer inserted into the centre of the cake comes out clean.

Turn out and cool on a wire rack.

continued

DECORATION

2 × 500-g packets white
   fondant

templates (page 225)

food colouring: green, yellow,
   orange, blue, pink, purple, red

2-cm flower cutter

knitting needle with
   rounded end

10-cm tall doll

5-cm round biscuit cutter

1-cm round piping tip

½ quantity royal icing (page 17)

flower stamens

1 round chocolate cake
   (page 149)

1 quantity mock cream (page 16)

fine paintbrush

white lustre dust

ASSEMBLY

Take a peach-sized piece of white fondant and roll out
to 4 mm in thickness. Using the template provided, cut
out the fairy's wings. Set aside the remainder of fondant
from this packet.

Divide second packet of fondant into eight equal
portions. Leave one portion plain and colour each of
the other portions a different colour: light-green, yellow,
orange, blue, pink, light-pink and purple. Roll out each
colour to 3 mm in thickness and use the cutter to cut out
as many flowers as possible. Gently push the rounded
end of the knitting needle into the centre of each flower,
to shape it. Set flowers aside to dry.

Take an egg-sized piece from the first packet of white
fondant and colour it yellow. Roll out to 5 mm in
thickness and use the template to cut out a dress for the
doll. Wrap the dress around the doll and join at the back.
Place straps over her shoulders and join to the dress.
Place doll upright and use the tip of a butter knife to
create the decorative pattern around the base of her
dress. Leave to dry.

From the white fondant, roll a log that is 3 cm long and
2 cm wide. Flatten at each end. This is the stalk for the
toadstool. Colour the remaining white fondant red and
roll out to 3 cm in thickness. Use the biscuit cutter to cut
out one round. Shape the round to resemble the top of
a toadstool (as shown in the photograph). Leave all
fondant decorations to dry overnight.

continued

Roll out a walnut-sized piece of white fondant to 3 mm in thickness, then use the 1-cm piping tip to cut out about 12 rounds. Brush each with a little water and stick onto the top of the toadstool. Use royal icing to stick the toadstool top to the stalk.

Place remaining royal icing into a piping bag and pipe small dots around the edge of the fairy's wings. Pipe a drop of royal icing into the centre of each fondant flower (colour the icing if you like). Cut a few stamens to length and use tweezers to carefully place them into the icing blob in the centre of one flower.

Cut the chocolate cake in half horizontally, to make two layers. Fill with ½ cup of the mock cream. Colour remaining mock cream green and use to ice the outside of the cake.

Use a fine paintbrush to apply some white lustre dust to the fairy's wings. Place the doll face down and use some royal icing to stick the wings onto the doll's back. Leave to dry.

Position toadstool and doll on the cake (as shown in the photograph). Use royal icing to stick the flowers all around the sides of the cake. Stick a few over the top of the cake, and stick the last flower (with the stamens) into the fairy's hand.

Football

 One day before: make the fondant grass
On the day: bake cakes and assemble

VANILLA CUSTARD CAKES

500 g softened butter

3 cups white sugar

6 eggs

1½ cups custard powder

4 cups self-raising flour

1 cup milk

3 teaspoons vanilla extract

METHOD

Preheat oven to 180°C. Lightly grease and line a
25-cm × 11.5-cm loaf tin and a 23-cm square cake tin.

Cream butter and sugar until light and fluffy. Add eggs
one at a time, beating well after each addition.

Gradually add sifted custard powder and flour and beat
well. Beat in milk and vanilla extract until combined.

Pour batter into prepared cake tins and bake for
40 minutes, or until a skewer inserted into the centre
comes out clean.

Turn out and cool on wire racks.

continued

ASSEMBLY

Note that this cake can also be made as a rugby ball, instead of an Australian Rules football – just adjust the shape and colour.

To make the grass, colour one packet of fondant green. Roll fondant into long thin snakes, about 6 mm in diameter, and cut into various lengths of between 4 cm and 7 cm. Taper off one end of each piece to a point, and flatten the opposite end.

For a third of the blades of grass, insert a toothpick into the flat end, leaving half poking out the bottom. Place grass onto a tray lined with baking paper and leave to dry overnight.

Carefully carve a football shape out of the loaf cake, tapered at the ends and round in the centre. Crumb coat the cake with basic icing.

Reserve a walnut-sized piece of white fondant from the second packet, then colour the remainder of the packet red and roll out to 7 mm in thickness. Carefully cover the cake with the red fondant, smoothing out any wrinkles and cutting off the excess. Secure with basic icing.

Using the template provided, cut out the oval shape for the top of the football from red fondant. Brush the back with a little water, then stick it onto the football (as shown in the photograph).

continued

To make the football laces, roll the reserved white fondant into snakes about 3 mm in diameter and cut into two pieces 2 cm long, and two pieces 3 cm long. Press the laces onto the oval on top of the cake, with the two longer laces in the centre and the two shorter laces on either side (as shown in the photograph).

With the back of a knife, draw lines across the top and around the sides of the football, to represent seams. Using a toothpick, dot along the edge of the oval fondant piece, to create stitches. Repeat this along either side of the seams.

Mix a small amount of black paste food colouring with some lemon essence, then paint along the seams and stitching to create the look of worn leather.

Level the square cake and crumb coat with basic icing. Leave to set, then place onto a cake board and cover the cake with chocolate buttercream. Place the football in the centre of the square cake, then carefully push the grass pieces on toothpicks into the cake around the football. Stick the grass pieces without toothpicks around the sides of the cake.

Motorbike champion

One day before: make fondant parts
On the day: bake cake, assemble fondant decorations, ice and assemble cake

CHOCOLATE CAKE

110 g butter

1 cup milk

1½ cups self-raising flour

½ cup cocoa

1 cup white sugar

2 eggs

½ teaspoon vanilla extract

METHOD

Preheat oven to 180°C. Grease and line a 23-cm square cake tin.

Gently heat butter and milk in a saucepan until butter is melted. Set aside.

Sift flour and cocoa into a large bowl. Add sugar, eggs and vanilla extract and beat until well combined. Gradually add milk mixture, beating until thick and smooth.

Pour batter into prepared tin and bake for 45 minutes, or until a skewer inserted into the centre of the cake comes out clean.

Turn out and cool on a wire rack.

continued

1 × 500-g packet chocolate fondant

5-cm round biscuit cutter

2 × 500-g packets white fondant

food colouring: blue, black, orange, red, green, yellow, pink

templates (page 226)

mini alphabet biscuit cutters

1 square chocolate cake (page 157)

1 quantity basic icing (page 15)

1 quantity buttercream icing (page 13)

lollies: 1 liquorice strap

toothpicks

coloured candles

ASSEMBLY

Roll out chocolate fondant to 15 mm in thickness. Use the round biscuit cutter to cut out two rounds for wheels. Set aside to dry.

Divide one packet of white fondant into two pieces. Set one half aside, then divide remaining half in two. Colour one piece blue and the other grey (using black colouring).

Roll out the blue fondant to 15 mm in thickness. Using the template, cut out the petrol tank from the blue fondant. Roll out remaining blue fondant to 5 mm in thickness, and cut out letters to spell MOTORBIKE CHAMPION. Then cut out two rectangular mud guards, each measuring 15 mm wide and 6 cm long.

Roll out the grey fondant to 15 mm in thickness. Cut out a 15-mm round and a 1-cm round. These will make up the motor. To make the handlebars, roll a snake from grey fondant that measures 7 cm long and 1 cm thick. Flatten out the middle section to make it 2 cm wide. Then roll a 2-cm ball, and gently press to flatten the top and bottom; this is the piece the handlebars will sit on. To make the exhaust pipe, roll out a snake that is 6 cm long. The snake should be 5 mm wide along the first two-thirds of its length, and 1 cm wide along the last third of its length. Roll out two more grey snakes, each measuring 5 cm long and 7 mm wide; these will be the forks (the pieces which connect to either side of the front wheel).

continued

Roll out the white fondant from the first packet to 5 mm in thickness and cut out four rounds with the biscuit cutter. Using a pizza cutter or sharp knife, cut each round into eight wedges. Cut out another piece measuring 2 cm wide and 15 mm long, for the front plate. Cut a 6 cm piece from the liquorice strap for the seat, and round the corners with scissors.

Divide remaining packet of white fondant into six pieces and make each a different colour: orange, red, green, yellow, pink and blue.

Roll out the orange fondant and use the template to cut out two racing stripes for the side of the bike. Roll out each of the other coloured fondants and use the template to cut out about 40 flags.

Using a little water, stick all the fondant pieces of the bike together (as shown in the photograph), and secure with toothpicks. Stick on the liquorice seat with some icing. Place bike on its side on a sheet of baking paper. Leave all fondant pieces to dry overnight.

Level the chocolate cake, then crumb coat with basic icing. Leave to set, then ice all over with buttercream icing.

When bike is dry, press a toothpick up into the bottom of each tyre, leaving half of each toothpick sticking out. Then press bike into place on top of the cake.

Stick the coloured fondant triangles all around the edge of the cake (as shown), and stick the letters spelling MOTORBIKE CHAMPION on top of the cake. Finally, arrange coloured candles on top of the cake.

Mermaid

VANILLA CUSTARD SLAB CAKE

500 g softened butter

3 cups white sugar

6 eggs

1½ cups custard powder

4 cups self-raising flour

1 cup milk

3 teaspoons vanilla extract

METHOD

Preheat oven to 180°C. Lightly grease and line a 38-cm × 27-cm slab tin.

Cream butter and sugar until light and fluffy. Add eggs one at a time, beating well after each addition.

Gradually add sifted custard powder and flour and beat well. Beat in milk and vanilla extract until combined.

Pour batter into prepared tin and bake for 45 minutes, or until a skewer inserted into the centre of the cake comes out clean.

Turn out and cool on a wire rack.

continued

vanilla custard slab cake
  (page 161)

templates (page 227–8)

1 quantity basic icing (page 15)

1 quantity buttercream icing
  (page 13)

2 tablespoons cocoa

food colouring: yellow, green,
  red, pink, blue

1 × 500-g packet white fondant

sea creatures Play-Doh cutters

non-toxic pastel colours of your
  choice

lemon essence

fine paint brush

edible markers in various
  colours

blue lustre dust

lollies: liquorice straps,
  1 packet cola sour tubes

ASSEMBLY

Use the template provided on page 228 to cut the body, head and two tail shapes from the cake. Crumb coat each piece with basic icing. Arrange pieces on a cake board and join with buttercream.

Put a third of the remaining buttercream into a bowl, add the sifted cocoa and mix well. Divide the rest of the buttercream into two bowls. Colour one portion yellow and the other green.

Ice the mermaid's body and head with the yellow buttercream. Ice the tail with the green buttercream. Ice around the sides and top of the head with the chocolate buttercream.

Take a fifth of the white fondant and colour it red. Roll out to 6 mm in thickness and use the templates provided to cut out the mermaid's shell bikini and her lips. Take a walnut-sized piece of white fondant and colour it pink; roll out and use the template to cut out the cheeks. Roll out a marble-sized piece of white fondant and use the template to cut out the eyes. Colour a marble-sized piece of fondant blue; roll out and use the template to cut out two irises. Roll out a peach-sized piece of white fondant and cut out five sea creatures with the Play-Doh cutters. Leave to dry.

Scrape some powder from the coloured pastels into separate dishes. Add a little lemon essence to each and mix to make a paste. Use the pastel colours to paint the sea creatures, and use the edible markers for outlining.

continued

Colour the remaining white fondant green. Roll out to 7 mm in thickness and use the template provided to cut out the two crescent-shaped pieces for the tail. From the remaining rolled green fondant cut strips 2 cm wide, then cut these strips into 4-cm lengths, and round one side of each rectangle (as shown in the template). These will be the scales for the tail.

Stick the crescent-shaped tail pieces into place. Arrange the scale pieces all over the tail, starting from the end of the tail and overlapping them like roof tiles (as shown in the photograph below). Dust the tail with blue lustre dust.

Place fondant eyes, cheeks, mouth and nose onto the mermaid's face, then stick on the bikini. Brush each iris with a little water and stick onto the eyes. Cut two thin strips from the liquorice straps, long enough to reach from the top of the mermaid's bikini to the top of the tail and stick onto the body (as shown). Cut a short strip from the liquorice, for the nose, and stick onto the face. Cut ten thin strips from a cola sour tube for eyelashes, and carefully stick on.

To make the hair, arrange the remaining cola sour tubes in curls around the face (as shown below).

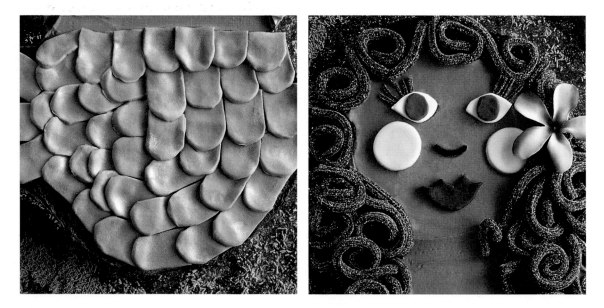

Treasure chest

continued

VANILLA CUSTARD LOAF CAKE

250 g softened butter

1½ cups white sugar

3 eggs

¾ cup custard powder

2 cups self-raising flour

½ cup milk

2 teaspoons vanilla extract

METHOD

Preheat oven to 180°C. Lightly grease and line a 25-cm × 11.5-cm loaf tin.

Cream butter and sugar until light and fluffy. Add eggs one at a time, beating well after each addition.

Gradually add sifted custard powder and flour and beat well. Beat in milk and vanilla extract until combined.

Pour batter into prepared tin and bake for 45 minutes, or until a skewer inserted into the centre of the cake comes out clean.

Turn out and cool on a wire rack.

ASSEMBLY

Level the top off the loaf cake. Cutting horizontally, slice one-third off the top of the cake – this piece will be the lid of the treasure chest; the larger bottom piece will be the chest. Crumb coat each piece with basic icing and leave to set.

Use the chocolate buttercream icing to cover the sides and top of the lid. Cut the liquorice straps into long thin strands and stick them around the edges of the lid, as an outline (as shown in the photograph). Cover the sides and top of the lid with cola straps (as shown).

Place the chest cake piece onto a cake board, then ice and decorate in the same way as for the lid. Arrange party favours and chocolate money over the top of the chest piece.

Place remaining chocolate buttercream into a piping bag. Pipe a thick line of buttercream along the back edge of the top of the chest, carefully place the lid on top of the chest, balancing it on the party favours and press down onto the line of buttercream at the back to secure.

Cut a keyhole shape from a liquorice strap, and stick it onto the front of the lid with basic icing. Finally, use basic icing to stick an aniseed ring onto the front and onto each side of the chest, for handles.

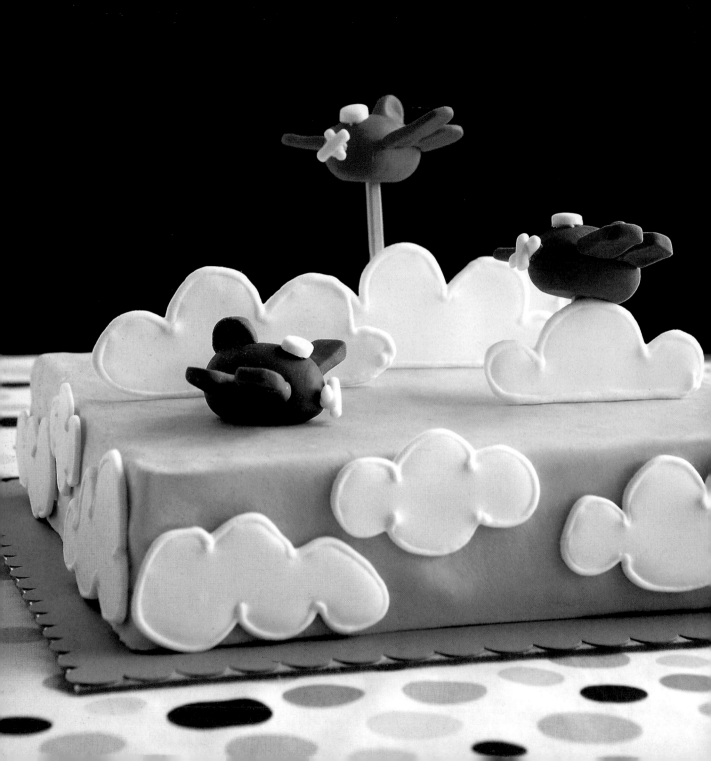

Up, up and away

One day before: make royal icing and fondant decorations
On the day: bake cake and assemble

CHOCOLATE CAKE

110 g butter

1 cup milk

1½ cups self-raising flour

½ cup cocoa

1 cup white sugar

2 eggs

½ teaspoon vanilla extract

METHOD

Preheat oven to 180°C. Grease and line a 23-cm square cake tin.

Gently heat butter and milk in a saucepan until butter is melted. Set aside.

Sift flour and cocoa into a large bowl. Add sugar, eggs and vanilla extract and beat until well combined. Gradually add milk mixture, beating until thick and smooth.

Pour batter into prepared cake tin and bake for 45 minutes, or until a skewer inserted into the centre of the cake comes out clean.

Turn out and cool on a wire rack.

continued

1 quantity royal icing (page 17)

templates (page 229)

2 × 500-g packets white
   fondant

food colouring: purple, yellow,
   green, blue

7-mm round piping tip

toothpicks

2 wooden chopsticks

1 square chocolate cake
   (page 169)

½ quantity basic icing (page 15)

ASSEMBLY

Place a sheet of baking paper over the cloud templates provided. Put royal icing into a piping bag and make 2 of each of the flat-bottomed clouds, and 4 of each of the other cloud shapes (see fill-in technique on page 6). Set aside.

Reserve an egg-sized piece of fondant from the first packet for later use. Divide the remainder of the packet into three even portions and colour each a different colour: purple, yellow and green. Make one plane in each colour.

To make each aeroplane: take a walnut-sized piece of coloured fondant and roll into a bullet shape for the body. Roll out the remaining coloured fondant to 4 mm in thickness and, using the templates, cut out two of each wing shape in each colour. Then use the 7-mm piping tip to cut out a round from each colour. Push a 2-cm long piece of toothpick into the flat side of each wing piece, leaving half sticking out (step 1, opposite).

Make the plane propellers out of the reserved white fondant. Roll fondant out to 4 mm in thickness and cut out six thin sticks 3 mm wide and 2 cm long. For each propeller, stick two of these pieces together in a cross, using royal icing to secure. Press gently where the pieces overlap to flatten slightly. Make three propellers, then use the piping tip to cut three 7-mm rounds from the white fondant for the cockpits (step 2, opposite). Leave royal icing clouds and fondant pieces to dry overnight. (Store leftover royal icing in the fridge.)

When fondant is dry, stick a propeller and cockpit onto each plane using royal icing. Stick a coloured 7-mm round to the top of each plane, towards the back (as shown). Carefully push the wings into the sides of each plane (step 3).

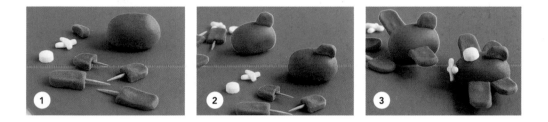

Use secateurs to cut the chopsticks to the desired length, discarding the thicker end pieces. Push the tapered end of each chopstick into the underside of a plane.

Level the top of the chocolate cake and crumb coat with basic icing. Place onto a cake board. Colour the second packet of fondant blue. Roll out to 6 mm in thickness and use to cover the cake, securing with basic icing.

For the clouds with flat bottoms, pipe a line of royal icing along the flat edge, then carefully position onto the top of the cake, standing upright. Use royal icing to stick remaining clouds around the sides of the cake. Position planes on the cake (as shown).

Love blossoms

 One day before: make fondant flowers
On the day: bake cake, make fondant branches and assemble

CHOCOLATE HEART CAKE

110 g butter

1 cup milk

1½ cups self-raising flour

½ cup cocoa

1 cup white sugar

2 eggs

½ teaspoon vanilla extract

METHOD

Preheat oven to 180°C. Grease and line a 23-cm heart cake tin.

Gently heat butter and milk in a saucepan until butter is melted. Set aside.

Sift flour and cocoa into a large bowl. Add sugar, eggs and vanilla extract and beat until well combined. Gradually add milk mixture, beating until thick and smooth.

Pour batter into prepared tin and bake for 45 minutes, or until a skewer inserted into the centre of the cake comes out clean.

Turn out and cool on a wire rack.

continued

1 × 500-g packet white fondant

2-cm blossom flower cutter

knitting needle with
   rounded end

non-toxic pastel colour:
   red, pink

lemon essence

very fine paintbrush

½ quantity royal icing (page 17)

food colouring: pink

flower stamens

1 chocolate heart cake
   (page 173)

200 g unsalted butter

200 g white cooking chocolate,
   chopped

1 × 500-g packet chocolate
   fondant

ASSEMBLY

Roll out the white fondant to 3 mm in thickness, and cut out 30 blossoms. Gently press the rounded end of the knitting needle into the centre of each blossom, to shape.

Scrape some powder from the red and pink pastels into separate dishes, and add a little lemon essence to each to make a paste. With the pink paste, paint the centre of each blossom; then use a very fine brush to paint thin red lines coming out from the centre of each blossom (as shown in the photograph).

Colour the royal icing pink and place into a piping bag. Pipe a drop of icing into the centre of each blossom. Cut the stamens to length and use tweezers to carefully place three or four into the blob of royal icing in each blossom. Set aside to dry overnight. (Store leftover royal icing in the fridge for later use.)

Level the top of the chocolate heart cake.

Melt butter in a heavy-based saucepan. Remove from heat and add white chocolate. Stir until melted and smooth. Set aside to cool until the chocolate mixture is beginning to harden but is still creamy in texture. Use the chocolate to ice the cake all over.

Take pieces of chocolate fondant and roll into about twelve 4-mm thick snakes of varying lengths. Arrange these branches around the edge of the cake (as shown). Pipe a little royal icing onto the back of each blossom, then stick them onto the branches.

Tropical fish

VANILLA CUSTARD CAKE

250 g softened butter

1½ cups white sugar

3 eggs

¾ cup custard powder

2 cups self-raising flour

½ cup milk

2 teaspoons vanilla extract

METHOD

Preheat oven to 180°C. Grease and line a 23-cm square cake tin.

Cream butter and sugar until light and fluffy. Add eggs one at a time, beating well after each addition.

Gradually add sifted custard powder and flour and beat well. Beat in milk and vanilla extract until combined.

Pour batter into prepared tin and bake for 40 minutes, or until a skewer inserted into the centre of the cake comes out clean.

Turn out and cool on a wire rack.

continued

ASSEMBLY

Level the vanilla custard cake, then use the templates provided to cut the required shapes from the cake. Cut fin pieces in half horizontally, and discard one half of each. Arrange the cake pieces on a cake board and join together with buttercream icing (but leave fins separate for now). Crumb coat the entire fish, and each fin, with basic icing. Leave to set.

Divide remaining buttercream into two medium bowls and two small bowls. Colour one of the larger portions yellow, and the other orange. Colour one of the smaller portions purple, and the other green.

Use the orange buttercream to ice the body of the fish. Ice the fins and tail with the yellow buttercream.

Place each of the four coloured buttercreams into separate piping bags. Pipe all the decorative icing onto the fish and fins (as shown in the photograph). Set aside to dry.

Use basic icing to stick the fins onto the body of the fish (as shown).

Cut the fruit rings into small pieces and arrange on the stripes (as shown). Stick on the Smartie for the eye. Sprinkle blue sugar crystals over the fins and at the base of the tail. Sprinkle yellow sugar crystals over the tail.

Hen and chicks

CHOCOLATE CAKES

220 g butter

2 cups milk

3 cups self-raising flour

1 cup cocoa

2 cups white sugar

3 eggs

1 teaspoon vanilla extract

METHOD

Preheat oven to 180°C. Grease one cup of a regular muffin pan and four cups of a mini muffin pan, then grease and line a 20-cm round cake tin.

Gently heat butter and milk in a saucepan until butter is melted. Set aside.

Sift flour and cocoa into a large bowl. Add sugar, eggs and vanilla extract and beat until well combined. Gradually add milk mixture, beating until thick and smooth.

Divide batter into one regular muffin cup, four mini muffin cups and the cake tin. Bake mini muffins for 8 minutes, regular muffin for 20 minutes, and the cake for 45 minutes, or until a skewer inserted into the centre comes out clean.

Turn out and cool on wire racks.

continued

1 round chocolate cake
(page 179)

1 quantity basic icing (page 15)

1 regular chocolate muffin
(page 179)

1 quantity buttercream icing
(page 13)

2 cups desiccated coconut

lollies: 3 white marshmallows,
orange sour straps, 1 liquorice
strap, green apple sour tubes

templates (page 231)

silver cachous

food colouring: yellow, green

4 mini chocolate muffins
(page 179)

1 tablespoon cocoa

1 × 100-g packet Chang's
ready-to-serve fried noodles

small flower sprinkles

ASSEMBLY

Level the top of the round chocolate cake and crumb coat with basic icing. Leave to set.

Round the edges of the regular muffin to make a ball; this will be the hen. Ice the muffin all over with buttercream icing, then roll in coconut to coat. Leave to set.

Snip the corners off each marshmallow (steps 1a and 1b). Use some buttercream to stick three of these strips onto each side of the muffin, in a fan shape – these are the hen's wings.

Use the templates provided to cut out the hen's beak, feet and comb from orange sour straps, and stick onto the hen with a little icing. Cut two small rounds out of a liquorice strap for the hen's eyes, and stick on. Use icing to stick a silver cachou onto each of the liquorice eyes.

Place remaining coconut in a zip-lock bag and add a few drops of yellow liquid food colouring. Seal the bag and shake until coconut is tinted the desired shade. Colour ½ cup of the buttercream yellow. Coat each mini muffin with yellow buttercream, then roll in the yellow coconut to coat. These are the chicks.

For each chick, use the templates to cut out feet and a beak from orange sour straps. Stick on with icing, then stick on cachous for eyes.

Put ½ cup of white buttercream into a small bowl, add 1 tablespoon sifted cocoa and mix well. Colour remaining buttercream green.

Place the cake onto a cake board and ice all over with green buttercream. Using the chocolate buttercream, make a roughly round shape in the centre of the cake, about 16 cm in diameter and 1 cm high. Scatter noodles over the chocolate icing to make the nest.

Scatter flower sprinkles around the nest. Cut apple sour tubes into short strips and place around the sides of the cake for grass. Carefully place the hen and her chicks onto the nest.

Day at the beach

CHOCOLATE CAKES

220 g butter

2 cups milk

3 cups self-raising flour

1 cup cocoa

2 cups white sugar

3 eggs

1 teaspoon vanilla extract

METHOD

Preheat oven to 180°C. Grease a Texas muffin pan, then grease and line a 23-cm square cake tin.

Gently heat butter and milk in a saucepan until butter is melted. Set aside.

Sift flour and cocoa into a large bowl. Add sugar, eggs and vanilla extract and beat until well combined. Gradually add milk mixture, beating until thick and smooth.

Divide batter into the prepared Texas muffin pan and cake tin. Bake the muffins for 25 minutes and the cake for 45 minutes, or until a skewer inserted into the centre comes out clean.

Turn out and cool on wire racks.

NOTE You will only need two Texas muffins for this cake, so freeze the rest for later use.

continued

DECORATION

1 square chocolate cake
(page 183)

1 quantity basic icing (page 15)

2 × 500-g packets white
fondant

food colouring: cream,
brown, red

new nail brush

2 Texas chocolate muffins
(page 183)

1 quantity buttercream icing
(page 13)

toothpicks

templates (page 231)

2-mm round piping tip

mini tin bucket

soft brown sugar

ASSEMBLY

Level the top of the square chocolate cake and crumb coat with basic icing.

Reserve a peach-sized piece of white fondant, then colour the remainder with cream food colouring. Roll out the fondant to 7 mm in thickness and cover the square cake. Place cake onto a square cake board. Press the bristles of the nail brush gently over the top of the cake, to give the fondant a grainy appearance.

To make the sandcastle, cut the tops off the two Texas muffins and then join them together with buttercream: cut-sides down and one on top of the other. Using a sharp knife, shave around the sides of the Texas muffins to create an upside-down bucket shape. Ice all over with buttercream, then cover with cream fondant. Place the sandcastle onto the square cake, near one corner, securing with toothpicks.

Divide reserved white fondant into two pieces. Colour one portion brown and the other red. Roll out the red fondant to 15 mm in thickness, then use the template provided to cut out a starfish. Use the piping tip to stipple indentations all over it (as shown in the photograph opposite).

To make the cone shell, roll a snake from the brown fondant, measuring 10 cm long and 15 mm thick. Taper one end, then curl into a spiral to make a cone shape (as shown in the photograph on page 182).

Roll out the remaining brown fondant to 15 mm, then use the template to cut out a scallop shell. Use the back of a knife to draw lines over the shell (as shown in the photograph).

Use a pastry brush to brush a little water over the sandcastle and the top of the cake, then sprinkle soft brown sugar over the sandcastle and cake, and on the cake board. Arrange the fondant decorations and mini bucket on the cake.

Blue planet

VANILLA CUSTARD PUDDING CAKES

250 g softened butter

1½ cups white sugar

3 eggs

¾ cup custard powder

2 cups self-raising flour

½ cup milk

2 teaspoons vanilla extract

METHOD

Preheat oven to 180°C. Grease two 15-cm pudding tins.

Cream butter and sugar until light and fluffy. Add eggs one at a time, beating well after each addition.

Gradually add sifted custard powder and flour and beat well. Beat in milk and vanilla extract until combined.

Pour batter into prepared tins and bake for 40 minutes, or until a skewer inserted into the centre comes out clean.

Turn out and cool on wire racks.

continued

DECORATION

2 vanilla custard pudding cakes (page 187)

1 quantity buttercream icing (page 13)

1 quantity basic icing (page 15)

2 × 500-g packets white fondant

food colouring: blue, green, brown

template (page 232)

lemon essence

fine paint brush

ASSEMBLY

Join the two vanilla pudding cakes together with buttercream icing, to form a ball. Trim the edges of the cake with a sharp knife, to get a perfectly round shape. Flatten the base slightly. Crumb coat the whole cake with basic icing.

Colour one packet of white fondant blue, roll out to 5 mm in thickness and cover the ball, securing with buttercream if needed.

Reserve two walnut-sized balls from the second packet of white fondant, then colour the remainder green. Roll out green fondant to 5 mm in thickness and use the template provided to cut out the map of the world. Brush the back of each green piece with a little water and stick onto the blue ball.

Roll out each of the reserved balls of white fondant into roughly round shapes about 5 mm in thickness for the north and south poles. Brush with water and stick onto the top and bottom of the globe. Place cake onto cake board.

Mix a little brown paste colouring with some lemon essence and use to paint the green parts of the cake (as shown in the photograph).

Three scoops

VANILLA CUSTARD CAKES

500 g softened butter

3 cups white sugar

6 eggs

1½ cups custard powder

4 cups self-raising flour

1 cup milk

3 teaspoons vanilla extract

METHOD

Preheat oven to 180°C. Lightly grease and line a 25-cm × 11.5-cm loaf tin and two 16.5-cm round cake tins.

Cream butter and sugar until light and fluffy. Add eggs one at a time, beating well after each addition.

Gradually add sifted custard powder and flour and beat well. Beat in milk and vanilla extract until combined.

Pour half the batter into the loaf tin and divide the rest between the two round cake tins. Bake the round cakes for 25 minutes and the loaf cake for 45 minutes, or until a skewer inserted into the centre comes out clean.

Turn out and cool on wire racks.

continued

ASSEMBLY

Level the top of the loaf cake, then use the templates to cut out the cone shape and the top ice-cream scoop shape from the cake. Use a sharp knife to trim the sides of the cone so that each side slopes in slightly towards the base.

Divide the mock cream into three medium bowls and colour each portion a different colour: pink, cream and lime-green.

Colour the white fondant with brown and cream food colouring to achieve the colour of an ice-cream cone. Roll out to 7 mm in thickness and cut into strips 2 cm wide, then cut these strips into 4-cm lengths and round the top of each (as shown in the template).

Using a little of the mock cream, stick these pieces all over the cone, starting from the top of the cone and overlapping the pieces like roof tiles (as shown in the photograph).

Cut a long 1-cm wide strip from the same fondant, and use mock cream to secure it around the base of the cone. Trim to fit and join the ends. Set aside to dry.

To make the ice-cream scoops: use a sharp knife to trim one of the round cakes until it is 15 cm in diameter. Ice with pink mock cream for the strawberry ice-cream. Trim the second round cake until it is 13 cm in diameter. Ice with cream mock cream for the vanilla ice-cream.

continued

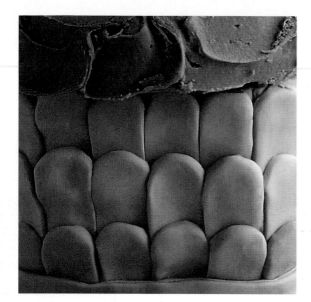

Take the ice-cream scoop shape cut from the loaf cake and trim the top with a sharp knife until it is 6 cm high. Ice with lime-green mock cream for the pistachio ice-cream.

Place the cone onto a cake board. Secure the pink cake on top of the cone using a little pink mock cream. Place the cream cake on top of the pink cake and secure with cream mock cream. Place the lime-green cake on top of the cream cake and secure with lime-green mock cream.

Push a skewer through the entire cake, from the top to the bottom, to secure.

Lamb chop

One day before: bake cakes and assemble (this cake is time-consuming to make)

CHOCOLATE CAKES

220 g butter

2 cups milk

3 cups self-raising flour

1 cup cocoa

2 cups white sugar

3 eggs

1 teaspoon vanilla extract

METHOD

Preheat oven to 180°C. Grease four cups of a mini muffin pan, then grease and line a 25-cm × 11.5-cm loaf tin.

Gently heat butter and milk in a saucepan until butter is melted. Set aside.

Sift flour and cocoa into a large bowl. Add sugar, eggs and vanilla extract and beat until well combined. Gradually add milk mixture, beating until thick and smooth.

Divide batter into four mini muffin cups and the loaf tin. Bake the mini muffins for 8 minutes, and the loaf cake for 45 minutes, or until a skewer inserted into the centre comes out clean.

Turn out and cool on wire racks.

continued

DECORATION

1 chocolate loaf cake (page 193)

1 quantity basic icing (page 15)

1 × 500-g packet chocolate
fondant

4 mini chocolate muffins
(page 193)

1 × 500-g packet white fondant

1 quantity royal icing (page 17)

toothpicks

silver cachous

food colouring: blue, black

bamboo skewer

ASSEMBLY

Cut a 7-cm piece off the end of the loaf cake for the lamb's head. Round the edges with a sharp knife. Then round the edges of the larger piece; this will be the body. Cut a small indent at the top-right corner of the body for the head to nestle into. Crumb coat each piece with basic icing.

Roll out the chocolate fondant to 5 mm in thickness and cover the head piece and the four mini muffins, securing with a little basic icing. Roll three sausages from the fondant, each about 15 mm wide and 3 cm long, for the tail and ears. Flatten ear pieces slightly. Set aside to dry.

Roll out the white fondant to 7 mm in thickness and use to cover the body-cake piece, securing with basic icing. Cut out two 15-mm rounds, for the whites of the eyes.

For the legs, place the four mini muffins onto a cake board and dab a little royal icing onto the top of each. Stick a toothpick into the top of each leg, leaving half of each toothpick sticking out. Position the body onto the mini muffins (as shown in the photograph) and press down gently.

Fill a piping bag with royal icing and pipe circular swirls all over the body (as shown). Place a silver cachou into the centre of each swirl. Use royal icing to stick the whites of the eyes onto the head.

continued

Colour small amounts of the royal icing blue and black. Place into separate piping bags and use to pipe the face onto the lamb (as shown).

Cut the bamboo skewer in half. Push both pieces into the base of the head, leaving half sticking out. Gently push the head into position on the lamb.

Use a little royal icing to stick on the ears and the tail. Leave cake to dry overnight.

Stellar ice-cream cake

🕐 **One day before:** prepare and ice cake, make fondant decorations
On the day: assemble

INGREDIENTS

4 litres vanilla ice-cream

2 × 20-cm round cake tins

1 × 200-g packet Tim Tam chocolate biscuits

1 litre thickened cream

2 teaspoons icing sugar

food colouring: blue, orange, pink, green, yellow

1-cm star piping tip

1 × 500-g packet white fondant

4-cm star biscuit cutter

ASSEMBLY

Take ice-cream out of the freezer and set aside to soften for about 10 minutes. (Remember that when using ice-cream, it's important to work quickly and refreeze the ice-cream as soon as possible. If the ice-cream starts to melt, return to the freezer for a few minutes.)

Line the two cake tins with cling wrap, leaving plenty of excess overhanging. Fill with softened ice-cream, pressing into the tins with the back of a metal spoon. Fill until ice-cream is 1 cm from the top of each tin.

Crush Tim Tams and scatter over one of the cakes, pressing the biscuit crumbs into the ice-cream with the back of a spoon. Completely cover the top of the cake with the overhanging cling wrap. Return to the freezer for at least 2 hours.

Divide the thickened cream into two medium bowls. Add icing sugar to one bowl and whip the cream until stiff peaks form. Chill. Add blue food colouring to the second bowl of cream and whip until stiff peaks form. Place blue cream into a piping bag fitted with the star piping tip. Chill.

continued

Turn ice-cream cakes out of the tins. Place onto a serving plate, one on top of the other, with the biscuit layer in the middle. Working quickly, coat the outside of the cake with the white whipped cream. Return to the freezer for 10 minutes.

Use the blue cream to pipe stripes across the top of the cake and down the sides (as shown in the photograph). Pipe around the top edge of the cake, then return to the freezer. Leave in the freezer overnight.

Divide the white fondant into four portions and colour each a different colour: orange, pink, green and yellow. Roll out each portion to 5 mm in thickness and use the biscuit cutter to cut out about 20 stars. Set aside to dry overnight.

To serve, brush the back of each fondant star with a little water and quickly stick all over the cake.

Templates

NOTE Use a photocopier to enlarge templates to the specified size. Dotted lines indicate placement. Shaded areas indicate how to place template pieces on whole cakes.

BOAT ENLARGE TO 200%

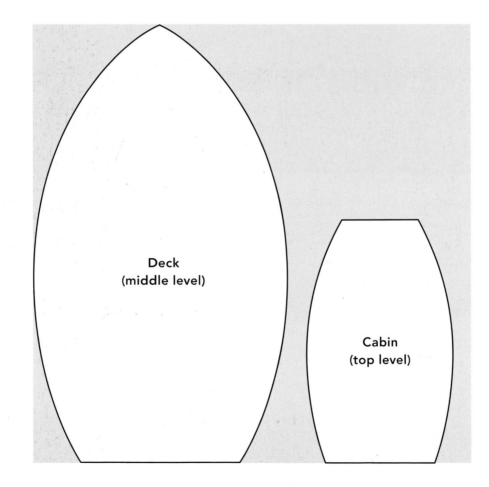

Deck
(middle level)

Cabin
(top level)

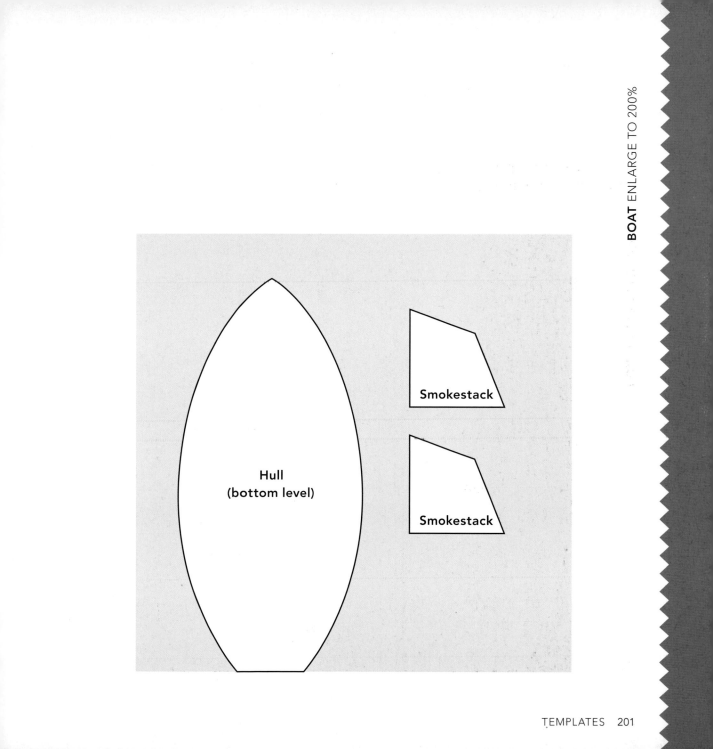

Hull
(bottom level)

Smokestack

Smokestack

Flowers, bugs and grass
Make 3 or 4 of each

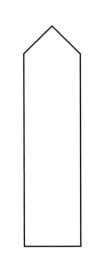

Fence picket
Cut 36

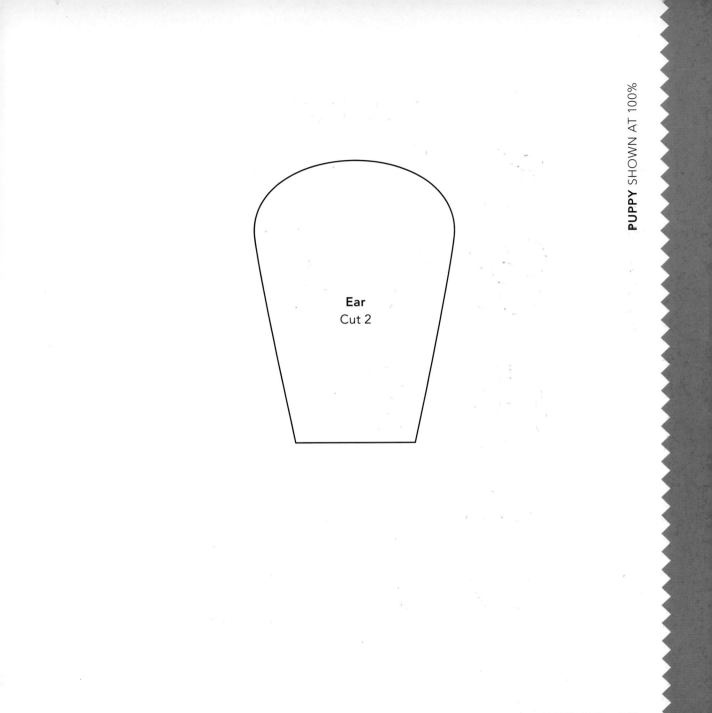

Ear
Cut 2

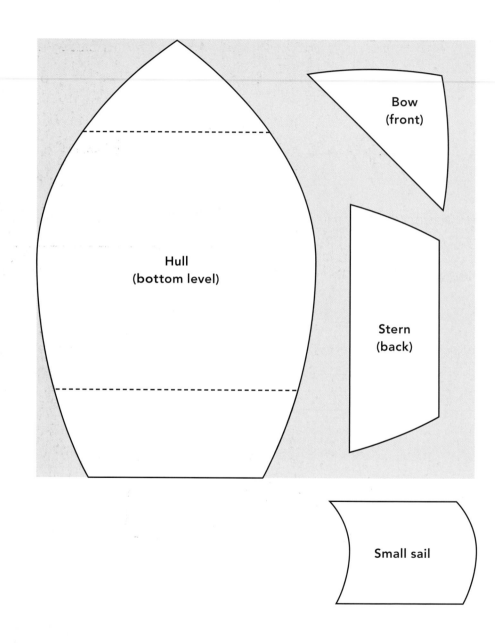

Bow
(front)

Hull
(bottom level)

Stern
(back)

Small sail

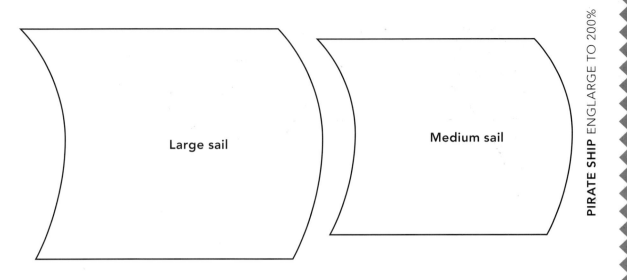

Large sail

Medium sail

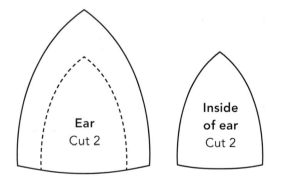

Ear
Cut 2

Inside
of ear
Cut 2

Torso

Bodice

Flowers
Make 10 blue and 10 pink

Wings
Make 20 pairs

Body

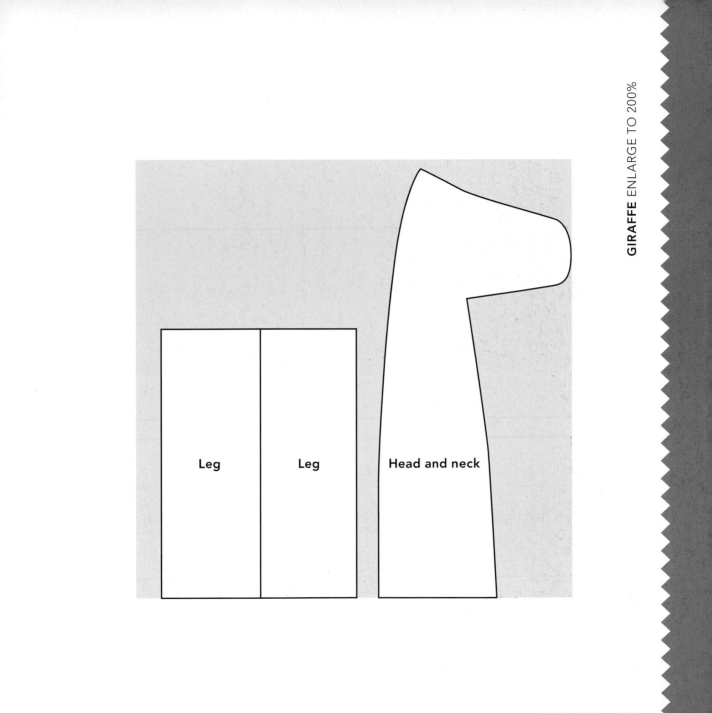

Leg

Leg

Head and neck

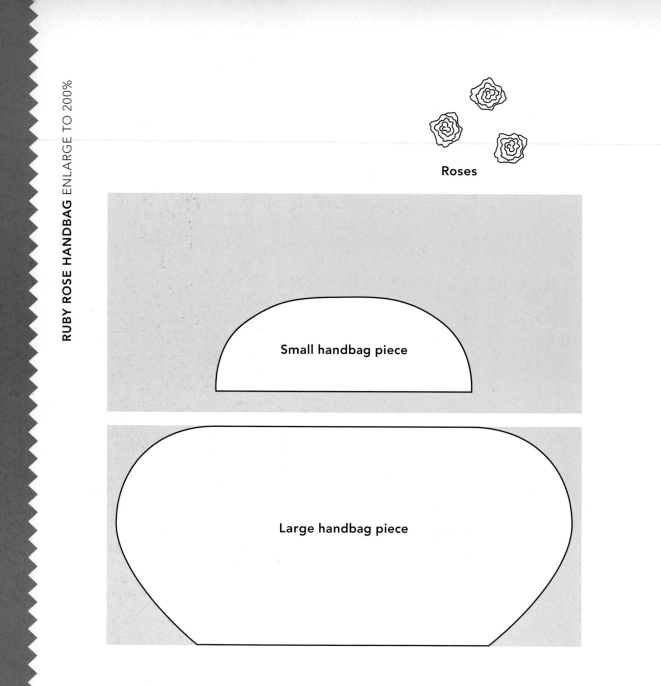

Roses

Small handbag piece

Large handbag piece

Tree trunk
Make 8

Leaves
Make 24

Grass
Make 10

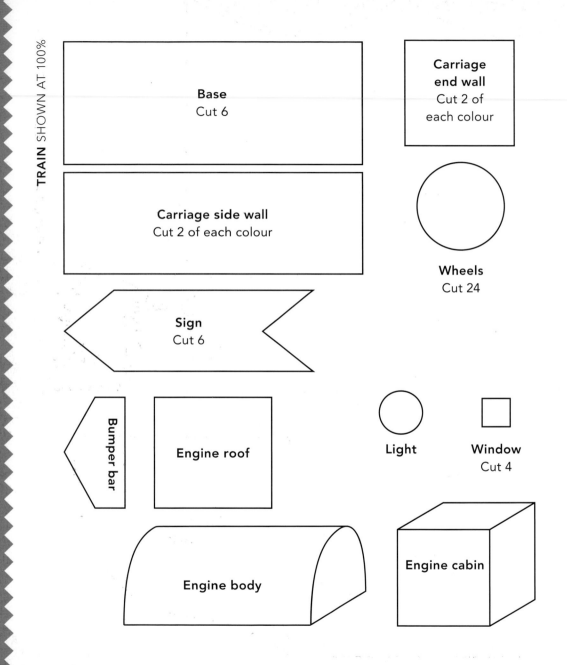

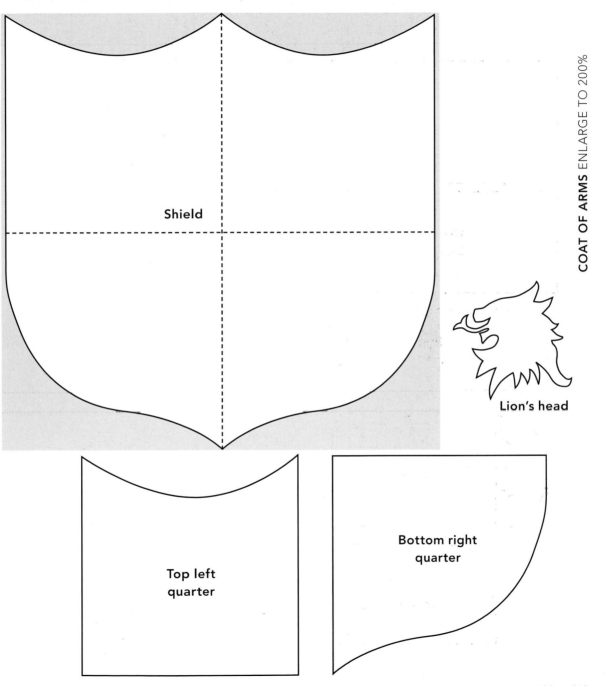

Shield

Lion's head

Top left quarter

Bottom right quarter

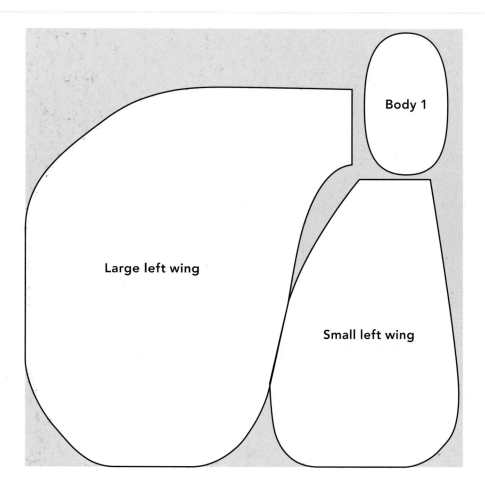

Body 1

Large left wing

Small left wing

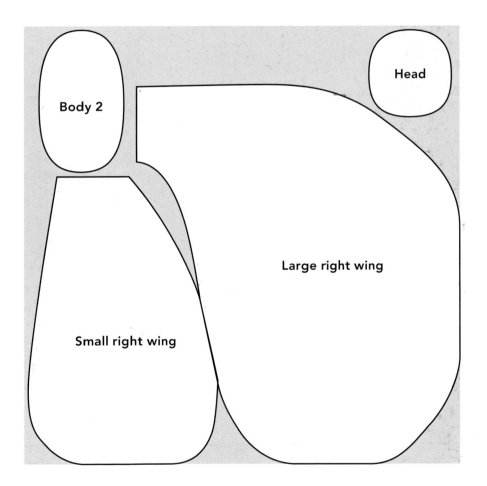

Body 2

Head

Small right wing

Large right wing

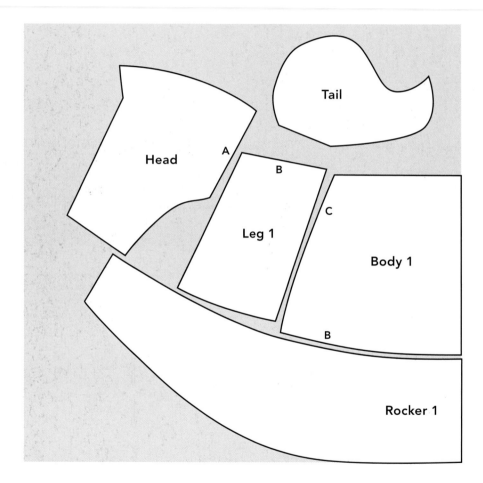

Tail

Head

A

B

Leg 1

C

Body 1

B

Rocker 1

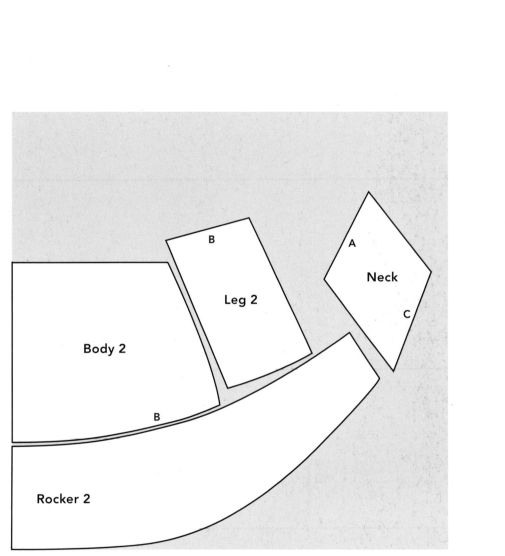

B

Leg 2

A

Neck

C

Body 2

B

Rocker 2

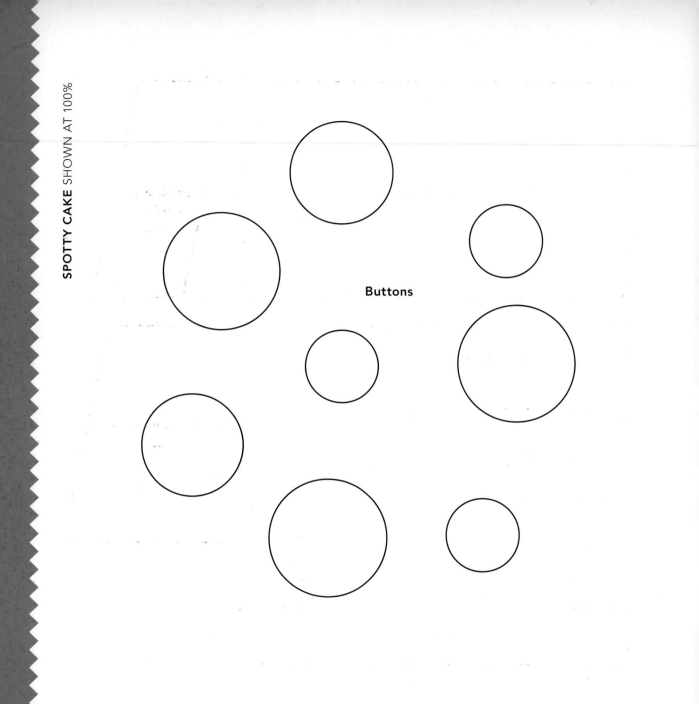

Buttons

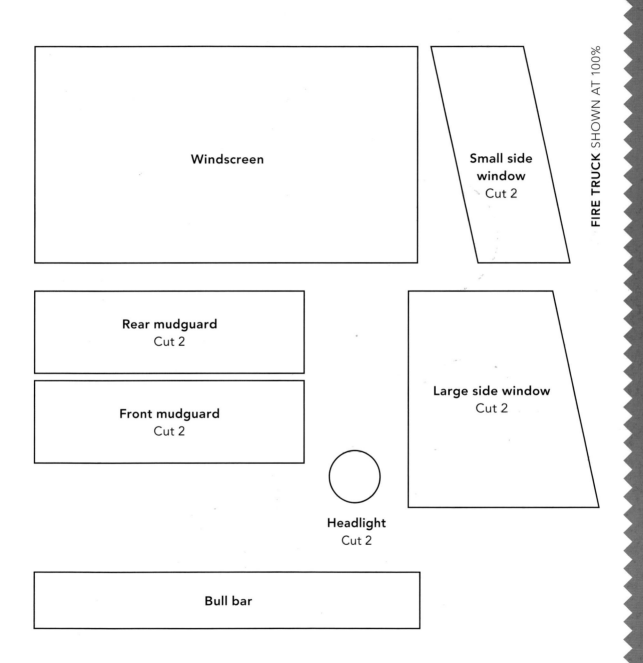

Windscreen

Small side window
Cut 2

Rear mudguard
Cut 2

Front mudguard
Cut 2

Large side window
Cut 2

Headlight
Cut 2

Bull bar

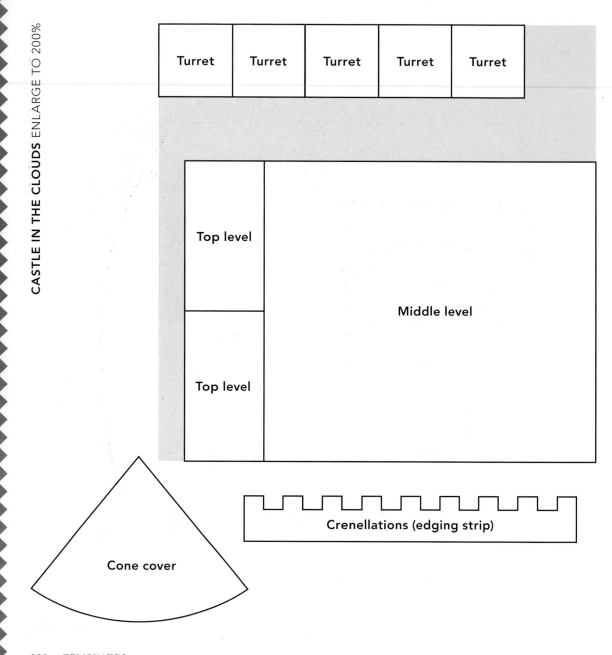

Turret Turret Turret Turret Turret

Top level

Top level

Middle level

Crenellations (edging strip)

Cone cover

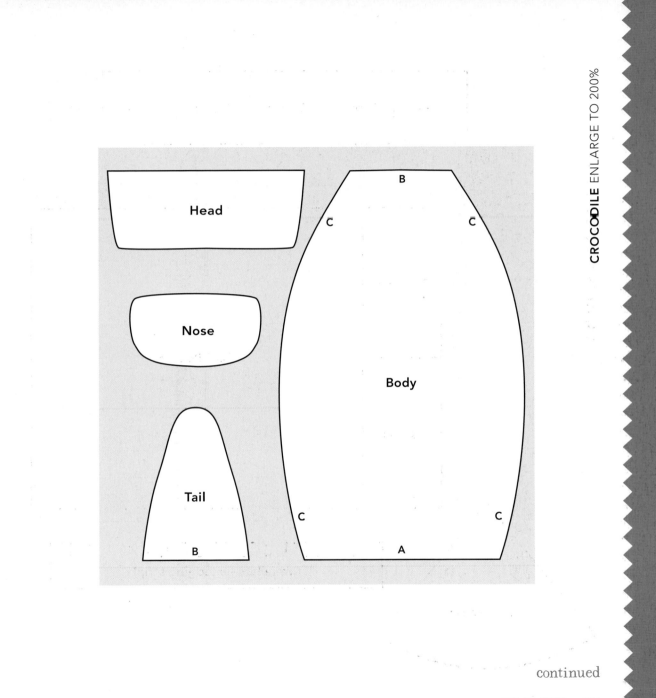

Head

Nose

Tail

B

Body

B

C

C

C

C

A

continued

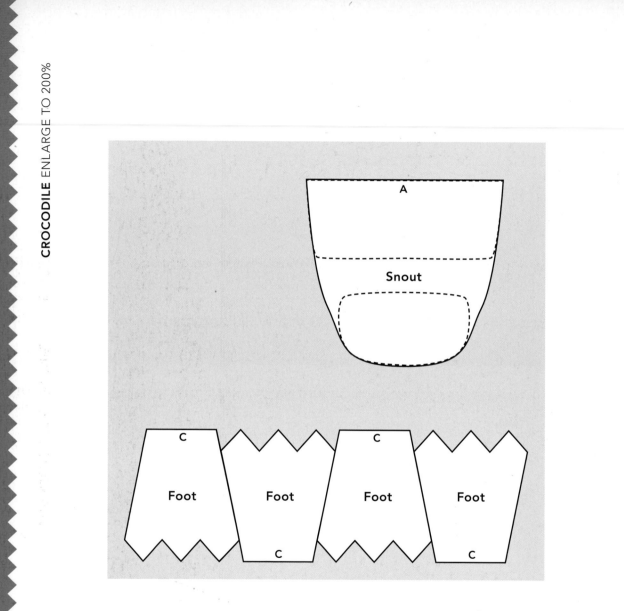

A

Snout

C   C

Foot   Foot   Foot   Foot

C   C

Rose

Boat

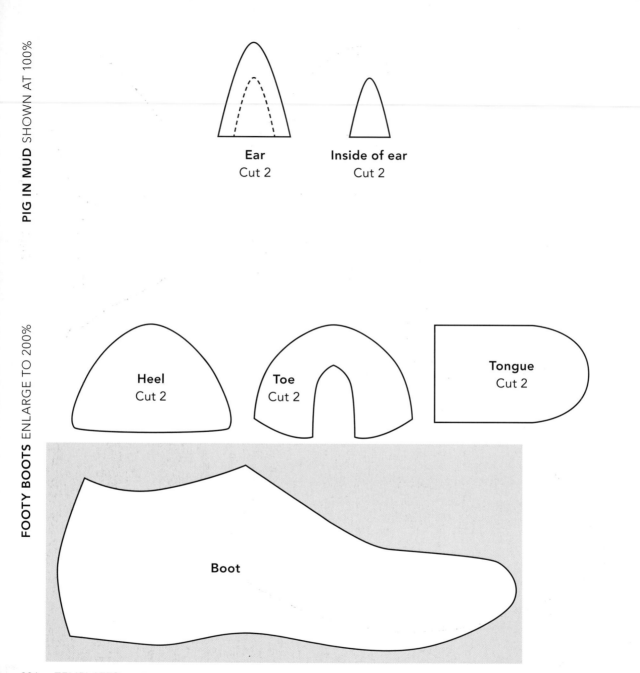

Ear
Cut 2

Inside of ear
Cut 2

Heel
Cut 2

Toe
Cut 2

Tongue
Cut 2

Boot

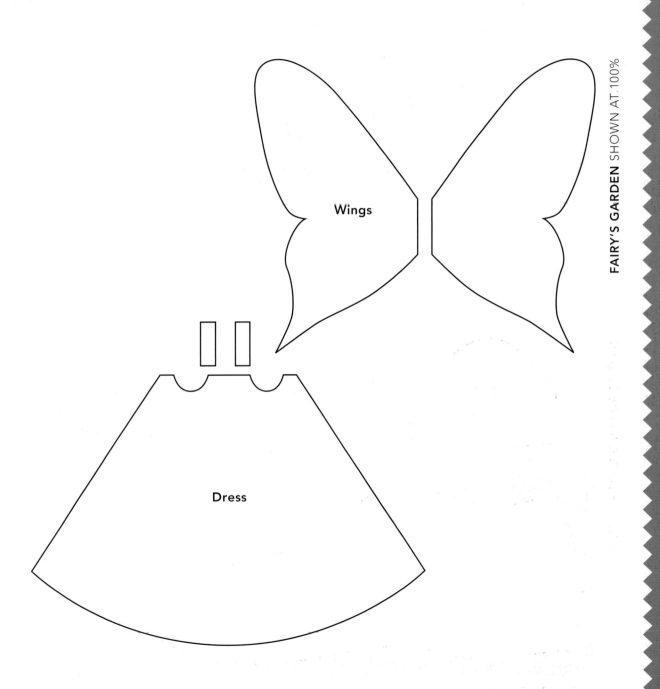

Wings

Dress

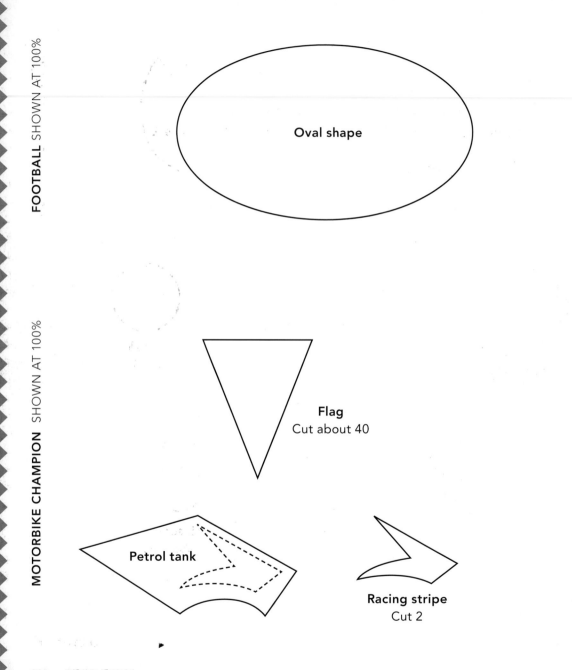

Oval shape

Flag
Cut about 40

Petrol tank

Racing stripe
Cut 2

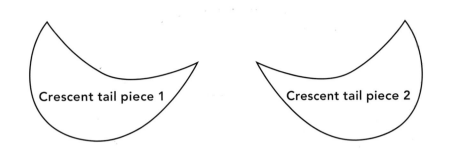

Crescent tail piece 1

Crescent tail piece 2

Shell bikini
Cut 2

Lips

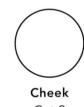

Cheek
Cut 2

Eye
Cut 2

Iris
Cut 2

Tail scale
Cut about 60

continued

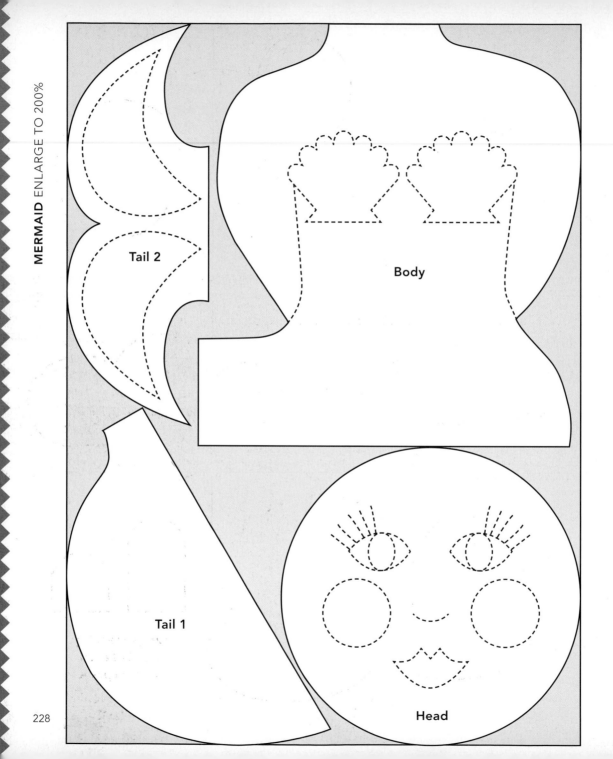

Tail 2

Body

Tail 1

Head

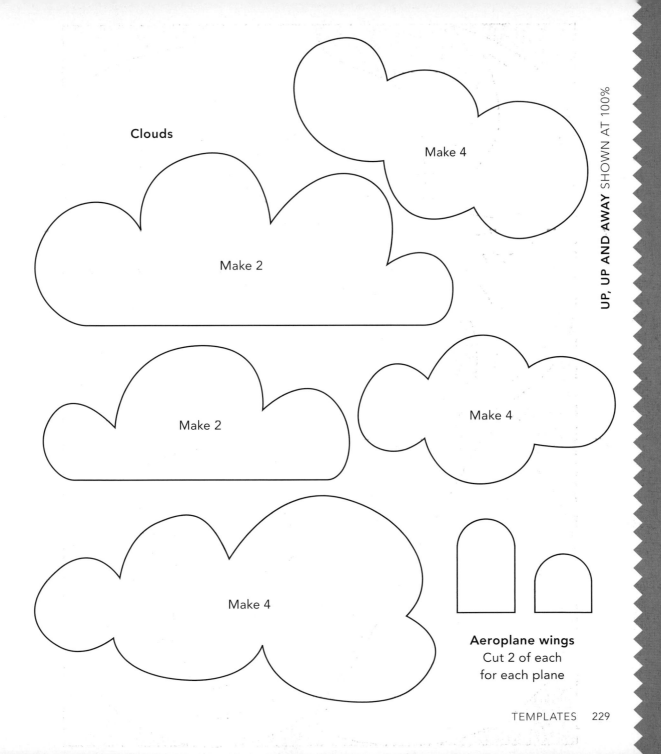

Clouds

Make 4

Make 2

Make 2

Make 4

Make 4

Aeroplane wings
Cut 2 of each
for each plane

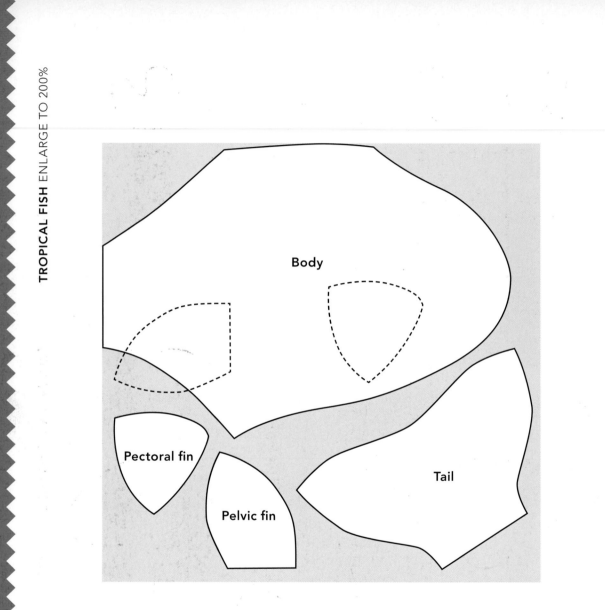

Body

Pectoral fin

Pelvic fin

Tail

Hen's feet

Hen's beak

Comb

Chicks' feet

Chicks' beak

Scallop shell

Starfish

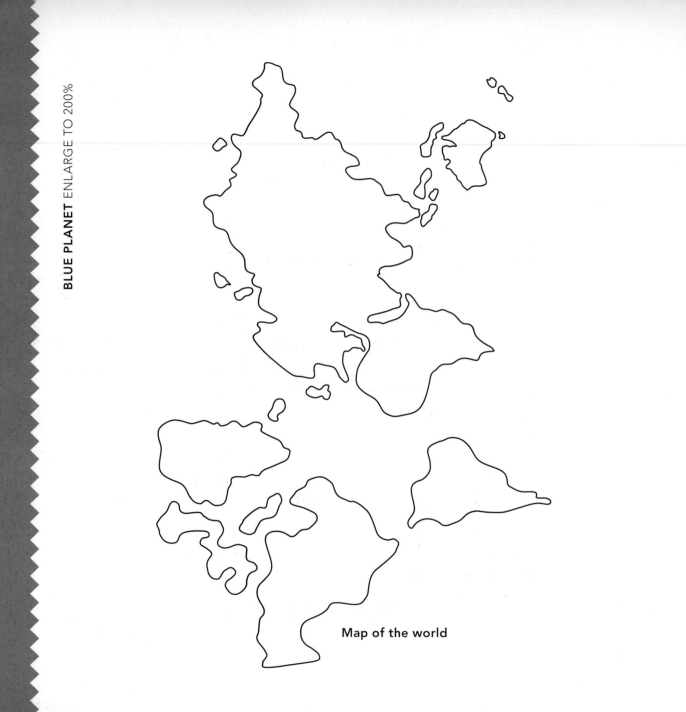

Map of the world

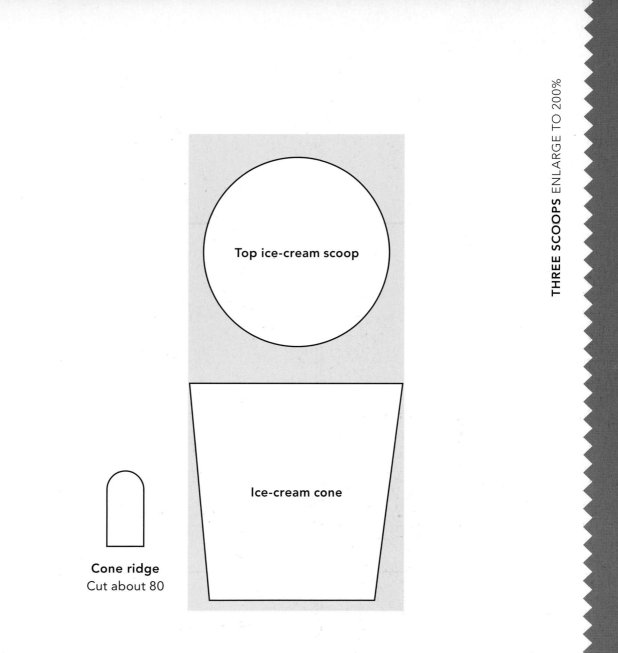

Top ice-cream scoop

Ice-cream cone

Cone ridge
Cut about 80

Suppliers

VICTORIA

ALLANS BAKERY AND CAKES
Shop 1, Kilsyth Shopping Centre
520 Mt Dandenong Road
KILSYTH 3137
phone (03) 9725 0926
www.allanscakes.com.au

BARBARA JEAN'S CAKE DECORATING SUPPLIES
Star Bowl Arcade
116 Fryers Street
SHEPPARTON 3630
phone (03) 5831 8600

CAKE DECO
Shop 7, Port Phillip Arcade
232 Flinders Street
MELBOURNE 3000
phone (03) 9654 5335
fax (03) 9654 5818
www.cakedeco.com.au

CHOICE CAKE DECORATING CENTRE
89A Switchback Road
CHIRNSIDE PARK 3116
phone (03) 9735 5375
fax (03) 9735 5365
www.choicecakes.com.au

THE ESSENTIAL INGREDIENT
Prahran Market, Elizabeth Street
SOUTH YARRA 3141
phone (03) 9827 9047
fax (03) 9520 3297
www.theessentialingredient.com.au

HOTEL AGENCIES
298 Nicholson Street
FITZROY 3065
phone (03) 9411 8888
fax (03) 9411 8847
www.hotelagencies.com.au

ICING ON THE CAKE
Shop 3, Corner of High and Sladen Streets
CRANBOURNE 3977
phone (03) 5996 7266

MARG & MAREE'S
54 Bell Street
HEIDELBERG HEIGHTS 3081
phone (03) 9455 1611
fax (03) 9455 0744

OLYMPUS PACKAGING AND PARTY SUPPLIES
13–17 Johns Street
LILYDALE 3140
phone (03) 9739 5735
fax (03) 9739 5963
www.olympuspackaging.com.au

WEST'S CAKE DECORATIONS

15 Florence Street
BURWOOD 3125
phone (03) 9808 3999
fax (03) 9808 5767
www.cakedecoration.com.au

NEW SOUTH WALES

BAKERY SUGAR CRAFT

198 Newton Road
WETHERILL PARK 2164
phone (02) 9756 6164
fax (02) 9756 6165
www.bakerysugarcraft.com.au

CAKE DECORATING CENTRAL

23/9 Hoyle Avenue
CASTLE HILL 2154
phone (02) 9899 3065
fax (02) 9620 4914
www.cakedecoratingcentral.com.au

CUPID'S

Unit 2, 90 Belford Street
BROADMEADOW 2292
phone (02) 4962 1884
fax (02) 4961 6594
www.cupids.idl.com.au

DUBBO CULINARY AND HOMEWARES

139–141 Talbragar Street
DUBBO 2830
phone (02) 6884 4468
fax (02) 6884 4473

HOLLYWOOD CAKE DECORATIONS

52 Beach Street
KOGARAH 2217
phone (02) 9581 1533
www.hollywoodcake.com.au

NEWTOWN PROVIDORES

62 Wingewarra Street
DUBBO 2830
Phone (02) 6882 0055

THE ESSENTIAL INGREDIENT

www.theessentialingredient.com.au

Shops 4–6, The Junction Fair, 200 Union Street
THE JUNCTION 2291
phone (02) 4962 3411
fax (02) 4962 3922

477 Pacific Highway
CROWS NEST 2065
phone (02) 9439 9881
fax (02) 8905 0678

15 White street
TAMWORTH 2340
phone (02) 6766 5611
fax (02) 67665367

473A Dean Street
ALBURY 2640
phone (02) 6041 4111
fax (02) 6041 4112

205 Summer Street
ORANGE 2800
phone (02) 6361 8999
fax (02) 6361 7950

ICED AFFAIR

53 Church Street (Parramatta Road end)
CAMPERDOWN 2050
phone (02) 9519 3679
www.icedaffair.com.au

AUSTRALIAN CAPITAL TERRITORY

THE STYLE EMPORIUM

Ginnindera Village, Gold Creek,
O'Hanlon Place
NICHOLLS 2913
phone (02) 6242 5223

THE ESSENTIAL INGREDIENT

52 Giles Street
KINGSTON 2604
phone (02) 6295 7148
fax (02) 6295 7146
www.theessentialingredient.com.au

SOUTH AUSTRALIA

ALL ABOUT PARTIES

78 Tapleys Hill Road
ROYAL PARK 5014
phone (08) 8347 2789

AUSTRALIAN CAKE DECORATION SUPPLIES

240 Magill Road
BEULAH PARK 5067
phone (08) 8331 9399

CAKE DECORATOR'S WORLD

15 Newark Court
GREENWITH 5125
phone (08) 8396 7272

CAKES ETC.

305C Payneham Road
ROYSTON PARK 5070
phone (08) 8362 7979
fax (08) 8362 7979
www.cakesetc.com.au

CAROLINE'S SUGAR ART SERVICES

Shop 4, 29C Dwyer Road
OAKLANDS PARK 5046
phone (08) 8377 0340
fax (08) 8377 0341
www.carolines.com.au

COMPLETE CAKE DECORATING SUPPLIES

Unit 1, 28 Eliza Place
PANORAMA 5041
phone (08) 8299 0333

QUEENSLAND

BB'S PARTY SUPPLIES & CAKE DECORATION

Shop 2, 481 Gympie Road
STRATHPINE 4500
phone (07) 3889 7547

CAKE ORNAMENT CO.

www.cakeornament.com.au

9 Counihan Road
SEVENTEEN MILE ROCKS 4073
phone (07) 3376 5788

Shop 7 Wilmah Street
ASPLEY 4034
phone (07) 3862 9542

Corner Kingston Road and Randall Street
SLACKS CREEK 4127
phone (07) 3290 0211

Shop 4, 51 Old Cleveland Road
CAPALABA 4157
phone (07) 3390 1588

MAKE IT AND BAKE IT

Shop 7, Margate Shopping Centre
266 Oxley Avenue
MARGATE 4019
phone (07) 3883 3444
www.makeitandbakeit.com.au

WESTERN AUSTRALIA

CAKE TINZ 'N' THINGZ

Unit 2, 6 Corbusier Place
BALCATTA 6021
phone/fax (08) 9345 1869

CLASSIC CAKE DECORATING SUPPLIES

Shop 16, Morley Market Shopping Centre
238 Walter Road
MORLEY 6062
phone/fax (08) 9275 7814

MAJOR CAKE DECORATION SUPPLIES

Shop 2, 900 Albany Highway
EAST VICTORIA PARK 6101
phone (08) 9362 5202

MY DELICIOUS CAKE DECORATING & SUPPLIES

Shop 4, 3 Lafayette Boulevard
BIBRA LAKE   6163
phone (08) 9418 5929

PETERSEN'S CAKE DECORATORS SHOP

Shop 8, 370 South Street (corner Stockdale)
O'CONNOR 6163
phone (08) 9337 9636
fax (08) 9331 5593
www.cakedecoratorshop.com.au

RAWJAC ENTERPRISES

Shop 43 Stephens Street
BUNBURY 6230
phone (08) 9724 1553
fax (08) 9721 2809

TASMANIA

BIRCHALLS

The Mall
LAUNCESTON   7250
phone (03) 6331 3011

CORYULE CAKE DECORATING AND CHOCOLATE MAKING SUPPLIES

Shop 7a, Bellerive Quay
BELLERIVE   7018
phone (03) 6244 1652

Glossary

ARROWROOT

A thickening agent that is wheat- and gluten-free. Can be substituted with tapioca flour. Both are available from the supermarket.

BAKING PAPER

A non-stick paper that can be used to line baking trays and cake tins. You can also pipe chocolate or icing designs onto it, which are easy to remove once dry. It can be reused many times.

BASIC ICING

A simple icing that is primarily used for crumb coating. It can also be used for securing decorations and fondant onto cakes, as well as for piping decorations.

BUTTERCREAM ICING

Used for coating many of the cakes in this book, it is a rich, thick, easy-to-make icing.

CACHOUS

Little edible balls used for decoration. They come in a variety of colours, including silver and gold, and are available in a range of sizes. They can be found at the supermarket and specialty cake decorating shops.

CRUMB COATING

A thin layer of icing applied to cakes before the outer layer of icing, to prevent crumbs from coming off into the topcoat. In this book the crumb coating is usually made of basic icing. To apply a crumb coat, ice every piece of the cake and allow to set before coating with your chosen icing.

FLOWER STAMENS

Edible stamens used to decorate flowers made from fondant. Cut the stamens to the desired length, pipe a blob of royal icing into the centre of each flower and use tweezers to place stamens into the icing.

FONDANT

A versatile pre-made icing that can be rolled out or moulded into shapes. Also known as ready rolled icing, ready-made icing or sugar-dough, it can be found in a number of colours in the supermarket and at cake decorating shops. White fondant can be coloured with paste food colouring and rolled out to cover cakes, giving a flawless smooth finish. Fondant can also be used for cut-out flat shapes, or for moulding three-dimensional shapes. Flat or moulded shapes can be made from uncoloured fondant and, when dry, can be painted with a paste colouring or non-toxic pastel colour that has been mixed with a little lemon essence. (*See also* Working with fondant, page 7.)

FOOD COLOURING
see Liquid food colouring; Paste food colouring; Oil-based powder colouring.

ICING TUBES
Small tubes of pre-made icing, sometimes labelled 'Writing Icing'. They are small, so there is little wastage, but this makes them unsuitable for larger icing jobs. Ideal for writing or outlining, they come in a number of varieties, such as solid colour pastes and clear fluorescent gels; however, the colour range is limited. You can find them in the supermarket. (*See also* Wilton's icing tubes.)

LEMON ESSENCE
A liquid that can be mixed with non-toxic pastel colours or paste food colouring to create food colouring of a consistency suitable for painting fondant. Because of its high alcohol content, the essence doesn't dissolve the fondant (the alcohol eventually evaporates). It can be purchased from the supermarket.

LIQUID FOOD COLOURING
Food colouring in liquid form is mostly used to colour icings. For a basic range of liquid food colourings, head to your local supermarket. However, if you're looking for a larger variety of colours, specialty cake decorating shops have over 20 shades to choose from.

MOCK CREAM
A very buttery, sweet cream that can be used for filling and icing cakes.

NON-TOXIC PASTEL COLOURING
A colouring that can be used in powdered or paste form. Similar in appearance to art pastels, they are scraped to create a powder, which can then be applied with a paintbrush to a decoration, such as an icing flower or fondant shape. Alternatively, it can be mixed with lemon essence to make a paste, and then painted on to white flowers or fondant.

OFFSET PALETTE KNIFE
A long palette knife that is fantastic for smoothing icing. Also referred to as an offset spatula, or a crank-handled spatula.

OIL-BASED POWDER COLOURING
Food colouring in powder form, primarily used for colouring melted chocolate. (Ordinary food colourings cannot be used to colour chocolate because the liquid makes the chocolate seize.) It can be purchased at specialty cake decorating shops.

PASTE FOOD COLOURING

Food colouring in paste form. It gives a much stronger colour to icing than liquid food colourings, and should be used in smaller quantities. It is more effective at colouring fondant than liquid food colouring and can be diluted with a few drops of lemon essence when painting fondant. You can also use it to colour melted chocolate. Available in a large range of individual colours or in sets of colours, it can be purchased from cake decorating shops.

PIPING

A technique used to decorate cakes with icing (see pages 4–7). The chosen icing is placed into a piping bag which has either a small hole cut in the end or a piping tip attached. Icing is squeezed through the tip to make patterns or letters.

POTATO FLOUR

A wheat- and gluten-free flour that is made from potatoes. It can be purchased from health food shops.

PURE ICING SUGAR

Pure powdered icing sugar with no additives. (As opposed to icing mixture, which has starch added.) All the icings in this book are made with pure icing sugar.

READY-MADE ICING LETTERS

These small, hard icing letters are great for adding words to your cakes. They're available at supermarkets or cake decorating stores.

RICE FLOUR

A wheat- and gluten-free flour made from ground rice. It can be purchased in small quantities from the supermarket, or in bulk from health food shops.

ROYAL ICING

An icing made with egg whites that dries very hard. It is used for piping fancy decorations and for fill-in work (see page 6).

SUGAR CRYSTALS

Coloured edible sugar used for decorating. Available in a variety of colours from the supermarket.

WILTON'S ICING TUBES

Tubes of pre-made icing that come in a great range of colours and have an attachment that allows you to use a variety of different icing nozzles. They can be purchased from cake decorating shops, department stores and some supermarkets.

Acknowledgments

To God the maker and giver of dreams, the creator who made us to be creative: I thank you.

To the man in my life, Rich, my husband, my own personal PA: you keep me going, keep me focused and make me feel like I can do anything. Thank you for standing beside me. You are my best friend. To my boys, Jack, Jacob and Elijah: this book is as much yours as it is mine, as many of the ideas and inspirations came from you guys. You rock.

To my family: how amazing to have a family that believes in you. Honestly, we do have such a great family. Thank you Lanhams, Thorpes, Phillipsons, Del Zottos and Scherers for all you do.

Thank you to Becky and Michael for letting me invade your home and mess up your kitchen as only I can do! Becky: you have been the motivator of lots of birthday traditions in our family, thank you.

Thank you Mum for passing on your love of cooking (and eating!) and family to your children and grand-children. Dad: thank you for all your ideas and phone calls – the way you get behind me has been a great support. To my other Mum and Dad, Rusty and Helen: thank you for making me feel very loved. Rusty, the Teddy Bear's Picnic cake is dedicated to you.

To my girlfriends, Jules, Tannie, Fi and my sister Sharon: what would a girl do without her girlfriends! Jules: you have been my constant source of encouragement and my bouncing board. Thank you for the years of friendship we have shared and for valuing my work enough to work with me. To my Tannie: you always inspire me to beauty and open my eyes to creativity, thank you. Thank you to Fi, your phone calls and emails and little parcels spurred me on.

To our Gilgandra family, a big thank you. This community has taken us in. Thank you for the ideas, the loaning of cake-decorating tools, supplier contacts and of course the cake testing.

Tania B: thank you for helping me make icing flowers; you are very talented. A special thank you also to Jess B: you are amazing! Thank you for being so excited about this book, your excitement for life is infectious.

Thank you to Kerryann of Dubbo Culinary and Homewares for all your help and support. Your shop has been a great source of wonderful kitchenware.

Thank you to Jo, Jess and Claire of Penguin. You are not only professional but very cool to work with.

Index